The Truth
behind the Broken

Samantha Wooler

ISBN 978-1-63844-765-8 (paperback)
ISBN 978-1-63844-766-5 (digital)

Christian Faith Publishing, Inc.
832 Park Avenue
Meadville, PA 16335
www.christianfaithpublishing.com

Printed in the United States of America

12 Years Old

And so, he did only a few miracles
there because of their unbelief.
—Matthew 13:15 NIV

Don't wait for miracles to occur to
jumpstart your faith. It starts with a slight
itch to begin your journey. Don't let the
creator of this world and your life pass by
because you are waiting for a miracle.
—The Daily Bible Devotion App

If you asked me what my favorite subject was in school, my answer would be English. Creative writing was like finding a piece of my soul out there in the world waiting to be told. Stories jumped off of every surface, crying out for their story to be told. That was my passion. Along with the writing piece comes the reading piece. I wanted to read every book in the world—to see the different stories come to life that were depicted in different versions than how I would tell them. I was a bookworm. I could sit for hours and read *Harry Potter*, *Goosebumps*, and *Nancy Drew*. The moment I could no longer make out the words on the page, though, my world crashed, halted, and spiraled out of control.

*****

"Cover your left eye please," the nurse asked me. I raised my left hand and placed it over my left eye. Blinking a couple of times, I tried to clear my eye of the haze that was in front of me. Taking my hand off, rubbing my eye, then placing it back on, I looked again. That same haze was in front of me, suspended in air. Then, swapping hands and covering my right eye this time, I was able to read the first three lines.

My mouth hung open at the shocking discovery that I could not see! For weeks, I covered one eye then the other. I was dumbstruck at how I could lose this much of my vision in such a short amount of time and not know what was happening. I tried to tell my parents, but they didn't seem all that concerned. "We'll see what the doctor says," they replied.

*****

Sitting in a musty brown chair at a vision facility, lenses were placed in front of my eyes one by one. The same question, "What letter do you see?" was repeated over and over again. I saw nothing. I saw no letters. Only big black blurs and hazy fogs that floated and danced their way across my vision. I was confused. My confusion turned into worry, and my worry turned into anxiety.

Following the doctor back to the waiting room, I stuck the tinted plastic glasses on my face and waited for the doctor to speak with my stepmom, Tonya. After having a discussion with the doctor, she walked over and gathered my three other siblings to huddle us all back into the van.

"Your father will not be happy. You basically wasted our money. She said you were lying and did not need glasses."

Tears began to form in my eyes. "I'm not lying," I squeaked out. The van door slammed shut. We drove home in silence as I watched the scenery flash by out of my hazy tear-filled eyes.

That night, I was told that I was grounded for lying. I knew I wasn't lying. I sat in my room on my bed with tears spilling out from my eyes. I tried to read my homework, but no words jumped out at me like before. Before, they danced and flew by as I read. I loved to read, so why would I lie about this? I couldn't imagine not being able to read. Lying down, I cried myself to sleep.

*****

School became harder. My eyesight became like a shadow dancing back and forth across my field of view. I could no longer see in the distance, no longer identify faces clearly unless up close, and no longer read. I shuffled my feet around in hopes to identify anything in front or to the sides of me in case I did not see it. My life was spiraling out of control. What once was a straight-A student was now a C-average student, and all my teachers noticed.

Final exams were upon us, and I had no idea how to pass them if I could not read them. Nudging my friend Nate, I bribed him with a pack of gum if he gave me all the answers to the exams. I felt pitiful. I was ashamed and humiliated at what I had to do to pass sixth grade. I saw no other choice though. No one believed me about my eyesight, so I had no one in my corner.

My report card came in the mail one hot summer day. My nerves bundled up, split open, and gathered again. This was it. I would find out if I completed sixth grade, or if I was to be held back due to my lack of vision. After watching my stepmom open the mail, I was told that I passed with a C average. Releasing a heavy sigh, I was happy to at least have passed. It was not my best, and my parents knew it; but I didn't care. I knew that I passed, and that was all that mattered to me in that moment.

*****

The time came when the next *Harry Potter* book was released. I was so excited and grew anxious not knowing if I would be able to read it. Deciding it was worth a shot, I had my dad and stepmom buy it for me anyway. Cracking open the hard cover, I peered into the book and waited for the words to jump out at me like they always had. Black little dots covered the pages. It was as if the book was made of black little specks of dirt and nothing else. I closed the book, took a deep breath, and reopened it. My eyes filled with tears. Curling into bed, I cried and cried, not understanding how this happened to me or what I did to deserve this.

In the presence of my family, I pretended to be engrossed with my book. I was afraid that if they didn't see me reading it, they would accuse me of wasting their money. So I pretended to stare at the words. In a way, I hoped that eventually my eyes would be able to make out the words, but nothing came.

On the weekends that I went to my mom's house, I had my sister Cierra read me my book. I was grateful that she was reading to me though at times she grew tired of it. Bribing her to read it to me was all I could do. I begged, bribed, and repeatedly asked her to read to me so that I could hear my favorite author's words and create my Harry Potter world in my head.

*****

As the summer weeks continued to pass, I began walking into walls and tripping over toys and big bowls of cleaning solutions; and I had to hold different objects, such as, bread, close to my face to be able to see them clearly. I was ashamed. My stepmom and mom began to notice. "Why are you kissing your bread?" asked Tonya. I became fearful of what others thought and wanted to hide in my room all the time.

My skin became itchy and cracked. It was as if my skin was shrinking on the outside, but I was expanding on the inside. Fear and anxiety were like a big ball growing and nesting in my insides. They were using my organs to nest, but there was no room. There was always a comment being made about how I was tripping, holding something close to my face, or spilling something. My stepmom or siblings were constantly there commenting on the new and different things I had to do due to my deteriorating eyesight. I hated it and became anxious. However, when I began hiding in my room, I would be asked about why I was in my room all the time as well.

*****

One weekend at my mom's house, Cierra and I were dancing and listening to music on the television. It was a regular thing for us. We were very close and always did things together when I went to my mom's. Due to our parents being divorced, we were the only biological siblings. We had others, but we were the closest. I asked Cierra what the song was called; then my mom stopped to look at me. "You can't read that?" she asked. I shook my head no, doing my best to ignore her look, and continued dancing.

*****

During our weekend camping trips, my mom walked into the hot sweaty tent to ask me and Cierra why we were not playing on the playground. Cierra replied, "I am reading Sam her book." I looked up at my mom and noticed her looking back at me.

"Why aren't you reading your own book?"

"Mom, she can't read it."

"Sam, you can't read it?"

Sighing, I gulped down my anxiety and told her that I could not. Walking away, she said she would make an appointment for me with her doctor.

The waves crashed within me, mixing, turning, and colliding. I was anxious but also relieved that someone knew the truth. I was excited to have told my mom. It was a sign that things would turn around. However, I was filled with fear and anxiety upon returning home to Dad and my stepmom. I was dreading what would happen when they find out that I went against their back and told my mom a different story.

*****

A little parking lot sat in front of a small rectangular building, where only my mom's blue van sat and waited. As my stepmother and I got out, my mom also got out of her van. Walking into the little building, my mom began the process of filling out paperwork and getting me checked in for my second eye appointment, only at a different location.

"Sam." My name was called. I followed a woman all the way back through the hallway and into the last room. Together my parents sat in the chairs pushed to the side as I again sat in a chair in the center of the room. Looking around, I saw all the same tools as I did from the first doctor's office. I became nervous and afraid that this doctor would also say that I was lying. Bouncing my knee, I quietly sat watching the doorway until the doctor came in.

An older gentleman with graying hair walked through the doorway smiling. He introduced himself and sat in the circular stool with wheels. "What brought you in today?" he asked. After explaining how I could not see or read, and after telling him the diagnosis of the previous doctor, he swung toward the machine to the right of my chair. He brought it forward and had me lean down and place my chin on the platform. Using a light, he went back and forth, looking into each of my eyes.

"Can you please tell me what letter that is up on the board?" he asked. I looked at the screen in front of me. I looked at it, willing myself to read it. I wanted so desperately to see it, but only a black blob formed in front of me. Shaking my head no, I replied, "No, I cannot see it."

Pushing the machine back into place, he prepared his materials to dilate my eyes next. He tilted my head back, and I watched as he hovered a white cylinder bottle above my face. He dropped two drops into each eye. I held a tissue to my eyes as they stung a little.

"Let those sit, and I will be back in fifteen minutes."

As he left, my stepmom turned toward my mom and said, "She's been reading her *Harry Potter* book."

"No. *Cierra* has been reading it to her," my mom replied.

After fifteen minutes, the doctor came strolling back into the room. Silently he pushed the machine back in front of my face. Back and forth, he went, shining a light into my left eye then my right eye. After repeating this motion several different times, he sighed and pushed his machine back into its home. Rolling back in his chair so he can see all three of us at once, he began his mantra of the end of my life.

"So the letter on the board was the big *E*, and I am not sure how the last doctor missed your optic nerves." We all looked at one another, and my stepmom asked the big question we were all thinking.

"What is wrong with her optic nerves?"

"Well, the optic nerves carry the blood flow to the eyes from the brain. They are supposed to be pink and gooey. However, hers are pale and cracked. I am recommending you to the Allentown hospital for a CAT scan immediately."

The next few things happened in a blur. The doctor called the Allentown hospital immediately and scheduled an appointment for a CAT scan of my brain. Getting into the car with my mom, we headed toward the Allentown hospital.

*****

I slid onto a hard white surface and waited for the machine enclosed around me to scan my brain. After waiting patiently, I got the scan over with and waited some more for the doctor to tell us the results.

Wearing a white lab coat, a male doctor came in and expressed his concerns over my images. He noted that there was a blood clot in the main vein of my brain; then, he strongly suggested for us to go to Children's Hospital of Philadelphia to see an ophthalmologist and hematologist for my vision and the blood clot in my brain.

*****

Together, my grandfather, dad, stepmom, mom, and I, climbed into my grandfather's blue SUV and headed to Children's Hospital of Philadelphia. My stomach pinched into tight knots. A wave of nausea over took me, and I could no longer hold the trembling of my lips. We waited in the waiting room for about forty-five minutes before I heard my name. I was taken back behind a blue door, where many rooms were aligned.

I walked into a similar room to the one I had visited previously. Then I sat in the large curved chair waiting for the doctor to arrive. In stepped an oriental-looking man with average height and dark hair and was wearing dark-rimmed glasses. He wore black dress pants with a button-down white shirt and a white doctor's overcoat.

My nerves began to grow from bunched-up balls into cocoons then into butterflies. They fluttered around in my stomach trying to escape. I gulped down some air, trying to push my nausea and anxiety down to the pit of my stomach. He introduced himself as Dr. Grant Liu, a specialist in ophthalmology and neurology. My family introduced themselves one at a time until it was my turn. I held out my hand, amazed to see that it was not shaking.

"Hi! My name is Sam."

Smiling, he replied, "Hello."

After the introductions, he began testing my eyesight. First, he handed me a little black book. After flipping to a page where orange and green dots swirled in a maze, he asked me if I could make out a number. I squinted my eyes tightly and held the book close to my face; I was determined to find a number in the colorful maze. Looking up at his expectant face, I replied that I could not see a number.

He flipped to another page then asked me the same question. Once again, I squinted at the maze; but this time, I could see a number. The colorful dots were different this time. Instead of them being green and orange, they were red and black. "Eight!" I replied happily. After flipping through a couple more pages, he took the book and sat it down next to him.

For the next test, he had me stare straight ahead at a television monitor. He played with the font size and put a letter up on the board. Unlike the last monitors I stared at, this one was more advanced. Dr. Liu could make the size as large as he wanted. Staring at the monitor, I only saw little black specks until he enlarged the letters. Finally, I could see a letter. "A, E, D, Q," I said. I felt proud of myself as I watched him nod in confirmation.

"Okay. Next I am going to have you take a field test."

Following two women, one tall and the other short, I entered another room all the way in the back of the clinic. The room had a giant cone-like object with a chair on either side of it. The two women went on the opposite side and asked me to sit in the black chair facing the open part of the cone. After giving me an eye patch, they explained how the test works.

"Okay, so the test will determine where your blind spots are and where you can see the most out of your eyes. Place the eye patch over your right eye first. When you see the light on the cone, press the red button."

Nodding, I placed the eye patch over my right eye first. Each time I saw the light, I pressed the red button as requested. Next, I placed the eye patch over my left eye and stared at nothing. I just sat there, doing nothing. After a few moments, both women stood and asked me to sit in the examination chair behind the large cone. After doing so, they tilted my head back in that familiar way and held the same white cylindrical bottle over my eyes as the previous doctors. After placing the eye drops in my eyes, they led me to the waiting room, where my dad sat waiting for me.

I needed some fresh air. So I put on the tinted plastic sunglasses that was given to me by the hospital; then, together with my father, I went outside to the front of the wood center. I could tell that something was wrong with my dad. He was quiet, and my dad was never quiet. I wanted a piece of his mind. I had not heard any results or opinions from the doctor yet, and I needed something to get me through the next part of this doctor visit.

He turned toward me and uttered the most terrifying words I could ever hear at that moment. "You have two weeks to live," he said. Apparently, given the location and the size of the blood clot in my brain, the doctor felt that I did not have much longer to live. Tears began to slide down my face. I hugged my dad, and together we cried.

My body went numb. I could not feel anything anymore. Together, my dad and I just stood outside embracing each other. Tears started to form in my eyes, but I tried so hard to hold them back. Focusing on the bus that was pulling up in front of the hospital to drop some elderly people off, I let my body go numb so I would not feel anything. I wanted to feel nothing. I wanted it to be so that if I were physically shocked, I would not even feel it. Placing layer upon layer of bricks upon my body, I built a wall that would cast out and away any emotion that I felt. These bricks would help me in staying numb and unaware of how I truly felt.

One last time, I was taken back behind the big blue door and into the room where Dr. Liu last saw me. He handed a card to my parents and told them that if they look through the first slot, it would be like seeing out of my eyes.

"So she has no peripheral vision?"

"No, what she sees is tunnel vision, except she has blind spots in her line of vision as well. In her right eye, there is nothing except light perception."

"What does this mean?"

"Samantha will need to learn how to adapt to being visually impaired. Her vision will most likely never come back."

"Glasses aren't an option?"

"No, being considered visually impaired means that she is partially blind. Her optic nerves are damaged, not her eyes. Her eyes are perfectly healthy, and unfortunately, in this time and age, we have not successfully transplanted optic nerves."

I didn't want to hear any more. I didn't understand why it was happening to me or even how this came about. Sitting in the curved chair, I just let the numbness overcome my body and prayed to the God I barely knew. I knew my grandfather and grandmother believed in him. So if they did, then he must be real. As I prayed, tears welled up in my eyes. I refocused back on to the conversation, willing them away.

"She will not be able to read regular-size font. Colors that she may confuse are the relatively close ones, such as, red, orange, yellow, blue, and purple. She will need to be very careful not to damage her eyes and lose any more vision than she has already lost." Then Dr. Liu handed a little white card to my dad. "Call this number to schedule an appointment with neurology. They can help reduce her headaches."

*****

I watched the trees dot the window as this time, my grandma, stepmom, and I traveled to CHOP. I waited in a different waiting room for only a few minutes before my name was called. This time, a woman with short dark hair entered the room. After reviewing my brain scan, she looked at my eyes then performed some reflex tests.

"I would like to admit Samantha in the hospital. Her blood clot is fairly close to rupturing, and I would like to examine her, get her a brain and orbit MRI with contrast, and see if we can prolong her blood clot from rupturing."

Hearing that I would be admitted was terrifying. I did not know what was going on with me, and from the sounds of it, neither did this doctor. I wanted to run to a faraway place, where I could die in peace. I hated being a test rat. I didn't want to be admitted. I knew that meant needles and shots and creepy, weird people coming into my room unannounced and unwelcome. I hated myself for what I developed, and I just wanted all of it to go away. Wiping the tears from my eyes, I said nothing. I didn't want to say anything because then, once again, that would show emotion.

"After examining Samantha's scans, it is determining that she has a blood clot in the main vein of her brain. What we would like to do is examine her and start her on a treatment to hopefully shrink the blood clot in her brain."

"Is this the cause of her vision loss?"

"We're not sure yet. At this point, you know as much as we do. We would like to keep her and evaluate her disorder and eyesight."

My skin grew even tighter. My head felt like it was going to explode. Now I knew why the first doctor said I only had a week to live. This blood clot in my head was about to explode. If that happened, I would be gone. I didn't know how to handle this. My dad promised that he would be with me in the hospital; but I felt alone, terrified, and cold.

*****

The next morning, a nurse who was carrying a silver tray woke me up. On it was a little white packet and a syringe. Smiling, she took my arm and told me I was going to be started on Lovenox today. Grabbing my upper arm, she pinched the backside, where some of the fat was, swabbed the spot where she was going to stick me then uncapped the syringe. After counting to three, she stuck the needle in my arm. Prickles ran up my arm, and I gasped in shock. It was more shocking than painful. She muttered a sorry then handed me a little cup of pills. I took them, muttered thanks, and closed my eyes to try and sleep again. Bustling around the bed, she took my vitals.

"The doctor ordered another MRI, so someone will be in shortly to take you," the nurse informed.

Fifteen minutes later, a young man came into my room and led me to a different part of the hospital. All the hallways looked the same. White walls; blue, green, red, and white floor tiles…We stopped at a gray-colored elevator, and the man pushed the down arrow. Once in the elevator, there was a voice that announced the floor number for each one stopped at or passed by. On floor 2, we got off. We walked down yet another hallway, and this one had a wall glowing with different colored lights: pink, blue, yellow, purple, and green. Each light had a different child facing you. The eyes seemed as if they were following me, and it was kind of creepy. I could not read the font, so I was not sure what was being advertised.

When we reached the other side of the hospital, I was taken immediately to a large room. In the center of the room sat a large cylindrical machine. Around it, the walls were painted blue. Various types of equipment lay around it on counters lining the edges of the room. The objects looked both familiar and unfamiliar, but it was partially because I could not see most of it. As I looked around the room, I realized that the farther away the object was, the harder it was to see.

I felt terrible. I saw children of all ages around me. I saw needles, machines, and doctors milling about. I wanted to scream and take all these sick children into my arms. I wanted to be okay. I wanted everything to go back to normal. I wanted to read, laugh, hang out with my friends, and see from far away. I missed when life was simple.

*****

Bright and early, a doctor walked into my hospital room to speak with me and my father.

"So we've received the results of Samantha's brain scan. After comparing her previous scan to yesterday's scan, her brain created new alternative ways to get blood flow to where it needs to go."

"What does this mean for Sam?"

"It just means that her body adapted to the blood clot in her brain, enabling her to receive blood flow to her optic nerves…just not as much as she needs. Also, we found a tumor wrapped around her optic nerve leading into her brain. We are not sure if the two are related. We will have to do some more tests."

My thoughts crashed into a wall of concrete. I was shocked that I not only had a blood clot—I now had a brain tumor. The only good piece of this news was how my brain adapted, making my life sentence possibly longer than the two weeks I had previously been informed about. It was a as if something in the world was watching out for me. I knew I should have died, but I was being given a second chance.

For a month and a half, I was tested and retested. The doctors were at a standstill and could not find any evidence of why I developed a tumor. They surmised that the blood clot developed because of the history of blood clots on my mom's side. The doctors decided that since they could no longer come to any conclusions or find anything new, it was safe for me to go home.

13 Years Old

This is my command: Be strong and
courageous. Do not be afraid or discouraged for
the Lord your God is with you wherever you go.
—Joshua 1:9 NLT

There may be times where we feel lost, alone,
and no one can relate to us. Trials can come
our way and sometimes we feel that no one can
help. Know this, God is with us wherever we
are and wherever we go. He is with us through
the good and the bad times even if we do not
want him to be. Sometimes hardships come
our way to sharpen us and make us stronger.
Next time you face a hardship turn to God to
lean on him and he will help you through it.
—The Daily Bible Devotion App

Depression was creeping into my body and soul ever so slightly. I
was growing tired of not being able to do the things I loved. My parents grew overprotective of me and obsessive over things that I could
and could not do, as well as the things I loved, like being with my
friends. It was becoming increasingly hard because the things I loved
to do, like reading my books, were ripped away from me. I was losing
myself, and I wanted to gain control of my life again.

Two weeks later, I was back in my grandfather's car. This time,
I was on my way back to the hospital for my angiogram and would
only have to stay for a day or two. After settling into my seat, my
grandfather began to mess with the buttons on the radio. I groaned,

knowing that this meant listening to the old Christian stations that he tortured us kids with for years.

"*Harry Potter and the Half-Blood Prince,*" a voice on the radio said out loud so I could hear it. My head shot up; and I looked at my grandfather in shock, amazement, and awe.

"You guys got me the new *Harry Potter* book on CD?"

"We sure did! There also is a CD player in the back for you."

I was ecstatic! I could finally listen to my new book and feel as if I am back in the Harry Potter world. My excitement was so overwhelming that I completely tuned out my grandfather's humming and disappeared into my own fantasy world. I was so thankful to have my grandparents. There were simply no words that could be said to show them my appreciation.

I clung to my CD player as I waited to be taken into the surgery room. I no longer felt nervous and scared since I was lost in the world of Harry Potter. I imagined myself at Hogwarts as part of the characters to allow myself to break away from the pain and the uncertainty of cancer.

Walking into another blue-painted room, I was taken to the familiar gray table that had taken over my short life. I lay my head back, and the nurse placed an oxygen mask over my nose. Wishing I had my book to escape from reality, I closed my eyes, counted back from ten, and thought of the book series that had encompassed my life.

*****

A white lab coat caught my eye as I was listening to my book. I paused the CD player and looked up at him. He stood in the doorway of my hospital room reviewing my chart. As he walked in, he smiled. "So your tumor is benign. It is known as a meningioma. You do not have cancer."

Relief came off me in waves. I was not riddled with cancer although I still remained an anomaly and still had a ton of medical problems. I knew, though, that this meant that I was able to go home and possibly back to school, where my friends were. For now, I felt like I won a small victory!

*****

It was a month after I left the hospital, and I was still not in school. My parents were worried that something could happen to me at any moment. I was ready. I wanted to see my friends. I wanted to live a normal life, and I wanted to go back to school. Day after day, I hounded my dad and stepmom about going back. They were worried about my blood clot, the tumor, my not being able to see my surroundings, as well as the bruises on my arms from the medication that were injected into me for my blood clot.

One night, while tiptoeing around the corner to the kitchen, I overheard my dad and stepmom talking about the principal placing me in a special-needs room. Tears flooded my eyes fast and began dripping down my face furiously. I didn't want to or need to be in a special-needs room. I could go in my old classes. I would just need some help reading.

"She doesn't need to be in a special-needs room."

"They don't want to have to deal with her or her disability. They have not dealt with anyone like her before. I am going to do my research and demand a meeting between all the principals and teachers. She has the right to be in a normal classroom setting."

*****

I was sitting between my dad and another older gentleman, whom I did not recognize, when a white piece of paper was passed from him to me. My dad took it and signed both his and my name. Once the paper was passed around to everyone at the conference table, the principal cleared his throat and began the meeting.

The principal began with who I was and how I became visually impaired. He spoke of how the school cannot help me and how I should be treated with special care since I am now a special student. After his speech, it was my family's turn to present their case.

"Samantha is an intelligent student who understands her work and is capable of working in a regular classroom setting. By law, you as a district are required to give her the help she needs. If this means buying her equipment or hiring an aid or vision teacher, then you are required to do so. I know she is very much capable of working well in a classroom setting, so she will be staying in a regular classroom setting."

As a result, the principal had no choice but to cooperate. By the end of the meeting, an aid was going to be hired to assist me until equipment and other things were purchased by the district to better assist me in being an independent student. I was delighted to hear that I would be returning to school and would be given help. However, I didn't realize that it was going to cost me something I was not ready to give up yet.

*****

Walking through the blue and white doors, I was extremely excited to see my friends again. Everyone was so happy to see me. I was caught up on some gossip, what has been happening around the school; and my friends and I stuck like glue the whole day. My depression lifted a little. I felt happy and whole again. I just needed normalcy and my friends.

The last period of the day was substituted with time with my new vision teacher instead of band. Walking into the classroom, I found that it was not a normal classroom. There were only a few desks, computers, and only one other student. The student was visually impaired and deaf, so he also had two other aids with him. I was introduced to everyone, including my new teacher, Mrs. Divornaky (Mrs. D for short).

We discussed my vision and how she could help me learn different techniques to overcome some of the challenges that I was facing. She also showed me different types of technology that could assist me in learning how to be independent again. For now, teachers would write things in on a big piece of paper in black marker. The words would have to be large and spaced apart so I could use the little vision

19

I had to read them. Mrs. D taught me how to use my fingertips to feel where liquid was when pouring a drink, feeling the edges of the steps with my feet since I could no longer see where one step began and ended, as well as how to use shortcuts on a computer to make it easier on my eyesight. It was incredible learning these new things. I needed this so I could try and be normal.

As I began to get accustomed to other students and the teachers assisting me, I began to feel like an outcast. I no longer could look at a textbook and work the problem out for myself. Instead of reading my own books, I had to befriend and rely on another person to do it for me.

I hated relying on others to help me or do the work for me. I felt ashamed, embarrassed, and unlike myself. I felt as if I was no longer a bright student but a person who used answers from others. I was no longer myself. I hated being this new person with this eyesight issue. I hated whom I had become.

*****

Browsing the many different types of Close Circuit Televisions (CCTVs), I saw old and new types of varying colors and styles. The older ones were nicknamed the old dinosaurs due to their being the first models. They were a musty white color. The TV screens sat up high, towering over my head. Down the back connected by a very thick rod was the X-Y table. The X-Y table sat underneath the screen and could move vertically and horizontally. This feature allowed for papers to be moved if you were to write or read the text on the paper more easily.

As I went from one CCTV to the next, I noticed that each machine was very different. Even though the layout of the newer machines were alike, some screens were clearer than others, others had better contrast features, and the rest just looked nicer. At the end of my tour, I saw the newest type of CCTV. It was a laptop with a camera connected to it by a USB port. This would allow for a high school student or college student to become more efficient and mobile. I wanted to be able to use the laptop and portable camera.

I thought it would be the best choice for me since I could not even read my own handwriting when taking notes.

When I had shown Mrs. D what I liked, she had told me the school district had already denied my getting a laptop. A little annoyed, I moved on to the next best thing. I would trial and error the CCTVs that had the monitor off to the side, was slimmer, nicer, and still had a camera attached to view the board in the classrooms. The only two downsides would be having to sit behind it and it not being so easy to move.

After Mrs. D and I returned to the school from our trip, a short Hispanic woman with short hair and glasses sat in the chair waiting for us. She was very pretty and had a huge smile. Jacky was to be my new aid, who would replace the students assisting me. She would go to each of my classes with me until I was ready to be on my own and independent again. We became close and not only as aid and student working side by side but also as friends.

[Sidenote: Here is what my eyesight looks from your perspective. Take a piece of paper, and cut out a tiny hole in the center; and where your peripherals are, stab a needle through the paper multiple times. This makes little holes where I can see if I move my eye slightly. Also, to give you a fuller perspective of my eyesight…I can see large objects around me; however, I cannot see from a long distance. If a person were to wave at me, I would not see it. I cannot read regular-size font, and I cannot see through my peripherals. And to watch TV, I have to be up close. I prefer to watch things on my phone because I can hold it as far away from my face as I need to.]

For weeks, Jacky and I did trial and error with many different CCTVs. To pass the time and make it fun, we nicknamed each CCTV. We made a list of what we liked and disliked. I felt better just being around Jacky. She was such a positive, beautiful, intelligent woman; and I loved her very much. Each day I saw her, my anxiety of being made fun of, not liking to sit behind the giant machine, and fearing that I couldn't see something, disappeared. Jacky was my light in a very dark tunnel.

*****

21

During the next couple weeks, I was determined to do my own trial and error on different CCTVs. I wanted to find the best CCTV for me. I needed to be able to see what was on the X-Y table as well as the board in the front of the classroom. One day, while messing around with one of our latest trial-and-error CCTVs, Mrs. D mentioned how it would be good for me to start learning braille. I knew that braille involved little clusters of bumps used to spell out words for visually impaired people to read. I did not quite know how it worked, and just thinking about it made my heart speed up. In my mind, I instantly thought, *No. One day I would have my eyesight back, and this whole nightmare would just become a memory.*

I wanted to be able to read my textbooks again. I missed the feeling of having a pencil in my hand, writing on a piece of paper. I missed seeing those little blue lines on the white paper indicating the lines within which a person should write. I missed my own personal books at home sitting on my now dusty shelf. The words, like little black dots now, no longer jumped out at me, engulfing me in the story. I needed to feel the fiction world again all around me.

*****

Mrs. D began to assist me in finding ways that I could accommodate myself so I could complete or perform tasks. Together, we went around the school to each staircase and counted the stairs to familiarize myself where the staircase begins and ends. Another trick I learned was how the railing on each staircase bent when the staircase began and ended. I learned to place the tip of my index finger inside my own cup when pouring myself a drink so it does not overflow. I had also learned to place a rubber band around my conditioner bottle so that I could distinguish it from my shampoo. I was learning lots of new things that could help me begin to get accommodated to my new eyesight. I began to learn more and more things as the days passed, and it helped me feel a little better.

*****

I finally chose a CCTV to call my own. It was clear, not as clunky as many of the others had been, and had a camera that I could place either on the X-Y table or on the whiteboard at the head of the classrooms. I was ready for school to be over. I always felt self-conscious about sitting behind the CCTVs and hated that I had to do so. It singled me out as different and held me apart from the rest of the class. Instead of sitting at a desk next to my peers, I sat at a desk with wheels, my CCTV perched on top, and to the side of the classroom. With this setup, I was out of the way of heads and eyes...and I was alone. I hated it and always wanted school to be over.

*****

Even though I had a CCTV to use so I could participate in my classes, I refused to use it. I hated sitting away from my peers. I hated being viewed as somebody different from everyone else. I hated knowing that I was different, and I had a hard time accepting that. Instead of sitting behind the desk with the machine that was supposed to help me be normal, I sat in the desk assigned to me if I were normal.

Jacky pleaded and asked me to sit back with her at the CCTV so she could help me, but I refused. I told her that I was fine and could sit with my classmates and follow along. I knew it was wrong of me to do, but I couldn't stand sitting in the back of class. I couldn't stand all the people around me looking at me.

Jacky went along with what I wanted and tried to help me as best as she could. I started to grow closer to her. She told me stories about herself, her son, and her daughter. I was jealous that she had such a good relationship with her daughter. I was a little jealous since I did not speak much to my own mother, and Tonya and I had a strained relationship.

Sometimes Tonya and I would get along great, but other times, I just felt unwanted. She had her children, and I believed that she wanted me to know that she was only my stepmom and nothing more. It was very strange, sometimes awkward; and I didn't know how to feel about it.

14 Years Old

I am bent over and wracked with pain. All
day long I walk around filled with grief.
—Psalms 38:6 NLT

Depression is a mindset. Once you enter that
mind set it is very hard to escape. David like
us was once depressed. It is very hard to escape
those thoughts that may engulf our minds like a
black hole. Remember God has a plan. Things
are put into motion for a reason. You are God's
child. He will take care of you and always love
you. For this reason, he has a plan for you.
—The Daily Bible Devotion App

The leaves began to change color. It went from being hot and sunny
to cool and colorful. It was a sign of fall coming, and it was my
favorite time of year. Cierra and I were across the street at the park,
talking, swinging on the swings, riding bikes, and enjoying the fresh
air. The sound of deep laughter broke our laughter as we looked over
at two boys around Cierra's age chasing each other. After them came
another taller boy around my age. Rushing toward us, they jumped
on the remaining swings next to us and asked if we wanted to play
tag or manhunt with them. Shrugging, we said sure.

"My name is Brandon," the much taller boy said to me. I smiled
and introduced myself. He was handsome, with short dark-brown
hair, chocolate eyes, and a smile that was charming and enchanting.
His charms twisted my insides, and I was joined to his hip. From ten
in the morning until nine at night, we were hanging out at the park,

smiling, laughing, and entertaining our younger siblings by playing games with them.

Sitting on the platform of the jungle gym, we cuddled, held hands, and smiled at each other. Cierra and the two others, Ryan and Justin, ran around laughing, making fun of us, and chasing one another. I slightly looked up at Brandyn and saw that he was smiling.

"I like you a lot, Sam."

My heart pitter-pattered. "I like you a lot too."

His eyes stared down at me, twinkling in the sun. Then he leaned down and brushed his lips over mine, asking if that was okay. Nodding, I replied yes, and our lips brushed once more.

*****

I was standing with my family on the sidewalk while we were waiting for the Halloween parade.

"You can go off with your boyfriend and your friends if you want, Sam," my dad offered.

Together, Brandon and I walked down the block. While looking for friends, I held his hand and let him lead me down few blocks. Noticing my surroundings, I realized that we were away from the parade area now and in the park. I followed, not wanting to disappoint him and thinking that we would be back in time as my father requested.

"Let's go to the movie theater and take our pictures," Brandon said.

I liked the idea, so I followed him without hesitation.

"I should call my dad," I said after a while. I tried the pay phone at the theater, but it was dead.

"We'll be okay."

I trusted my boyfriend; so we just took pictures of the two of us laughing, smiling, and kissing. Together, we slipped into the dark, empty theater, where no movie was playing.

"Let's just sit here and kiss," Brandon said.

Hands began to roam all over me. Grasping my chest, cupping places that no person should be cupped. Then he unzipped my pants and rubbed himself all over me. I gasped, trying to say the word *no*, but my cries were silenced by his kisses. I didn't understand what was happening. I understood what he wanted, but I could not fathom that my boyfriend would do such a thing to me. I cried and pushed away from him. I felt numb and paralyzed, and I didn't know what to do. After pulling up my pants, we walked out of the theater, and I began my walk home.

*****

"Dad's been looking all over for you," Hali said as I walked into the house. Both my parents were gone, and only my siblings were home. I did not reply to her and just waited for my dad to come home. I wanted to tell him everything that happened; but I became afraid that If I did, he would go to Brandon's house and do something terrible. Slamming the door shut, my dad stomped over and slapped me across the face. Stumbling back, I was shocked that he would do so without even asking me where I was. Tears slid down my face as I put a palm to my burning cheek. Not wanting to say anything now, I just stood there and let him yell and scream at me.

The next morning, it was my stepmom's turn. She woke up before I went to school, and again, I was slapped across the face. They repeatedly asked me where I was. I told them that I had gone to the theater and then home. I told them I tried to call; but when they found the pictures, they didn't believe me. Being slapped twice in less than twenty-four hours, I was afraid I would have a permanent red mark on my face. Terrified to even say a word, I hid within myself and took the verbal and physical assault.

*****

Days went by, and I was constantly bombarded with questions about what exactly had occurred during the time I was missing. They wanted to know how I ended up at the theater, how we got pictures taken, and how I ended up at home. My head hurt from the constant harassment. Each time I gave them an answer, though, I was called a liar, a slut, stupid, and dumb. These words snuck into my brain, infiltrating my soul, spirit, and heart. Tears made their way down my face each night before sleeping. And sadness slowly crept over my weary body, nesting in my soul.

Each weekend I was at my mom's house, I got a break from the yelling, questioning, and name-calling. I was not harassed for answers, and I did not feel isolated from anyone—I could be myself again. I tried to call Brandon for some answers, but he always ignored my phone calls. I couldn't understand what happened, why he would do such a thing to me, or why he was ignoring me. Something felt off, and I wanted some type of answer as to why. I tried every weekend I went to my mom's house; but each time, it was always the same. I slowly began to understand that I was used for something he wanted from me; then I was tossed away into the trash as if I meant nothing to him.

*****

Stupid, dumb, like your mother, unforgivable, not to be trusted... These were all words that repeated constantly around me. The isolation from having no friends around, not being able to simply go outside, or only allowed home alone or with siblings, were all things that I've had to deal with. Instead of being grounded for a couple weeks, I was grounded for three months. The total isolation, name-calling, and harassment killed me on the inside. I became nothing. Just a body that acted automatically to what I knew I was supposed to do and retreated from what I was not supposed to do.

Each day I came home from school, I did my homework and sat on the ground watching TV. It sickened me to mindlessly watch television. I'd rather read. However, I was not allowed in my room, nor did I have many books I could listen to. I was stuck in the living room with the rest of my siblings and Tonya each day. My personal likes became obsolete. Depression was created, and the darkness covered my eyes.

*****

"Taking her wrist and sliding it across the sharp edges of the paper towel dispenser…" I sat listening to a book that I had to read for English class. The girl was in a hospital and cutting her wrist on the sharpened spot of the paper-towel dispenser to release her inner pain. Listening to the book gave me chills. The wheels in my brain began to turn and click together as I processed her feelings. The pain seeped out of her with the droplets of blood that was released from her own body by cutting her wrist…

Standing in front of the bathroom sink at home, I took my banana-yellow razor. Running my thumb over the edge, I felt the sharpness. There was no light left for me to clutch on to. Instead, only darkness remained, and I wanted a way out so bad. The constant name-calling from both Tonya and my dad were becoming too much. Idiot, stupid, dumb, retard…those were all the names that were now part of my identity. Not sister, not daughter…Not happy. There was only rejection, disappointment, and self-loathing. I was becoming weary. My body and mind ached from the loathing they had on me as well as the loathing I had for myself.

I wiped my tears away and swiped the blade across my wrist. The sharp sting let me finally feel something. Watching the blood gather on my wrist, I let it splash down to the white sink. I turned the faucet on to wash away the evidence and repeated the process. I help the razor once more and swiped it against the already-marked skin of my wrist. I watched more blood gather, rinsed it with cold water, and felt more stinging sensations. I could feel my tears and sadness wash away with the blood. Together they mingled and disappeared down the drain.

*****

Redness splattered the bathtub as I showered. There was no feeling left. I no longer felt the sting of the razor biting my skin, so I began slicing more and more. Tears no longer took residence in my eyes; and I became silent, unfeeling, and unmoved. I no longer said anything to anyone. At school, I just sat there listening to my friends talk but never joined in myself. I was truly engulfed in the darkness now. There was nothing left. I was neither here nor there, and I was not important enough for anyone to even realize something was wrong.

"SAM!" my father shouted for me one weekend while Cierra was visiting. I stomped up the basement stairs and walked into the living room, where my dad sat in front of the computer. Looking at the screen, I saw the big block letters that spelled eBay. Hali, Cierra, and Brianna were also gathered around the computer as I stood waiting for my dad to say something.

"I found something on the Internet you guys might be interested in. It is a way to speak to spirits through a board called the Ouija board."

Cierra and Hali looked at each other. "How does it work?"

"You sit in a circle and put two fingers on a piece of the board. A spirit then moves that piece around to a certain letter or word so it can talk to you."

*****

Cierra, Hali, Brianna, Dad, and I all sat on the floor while Dad set out flowers, a bowl of water, some salt, and the board that he bought off of eBay. He, Cierra, and Hali sat around the board, inviting spirits into our home and asking them to speak with them through the board. Brianna and I sat on the couch watching as the triangular planchet moved around the board answering their questions.

As weeks went by, Hali, Cierra, and I constantly wanted to try the board that would allow us to talk to spirits. We invited spirits into our home to talk to us. I desperately wanted attention from something. I wanted to connect and not feel nothing at all anymore. I was ready to have my emotions, feelings, and thoughts spin, turn, and connect with other thoughts and feelings. It was no use though. Each time I was picked on, scolded, or punished, I would return to the bathroom and become reacquainted with my razor.

Sitting on the toilet, I began to hyperventilate. I felt like my insides were burning up. I wanted to claw out of my body and be free. Putting my head on the cool surface of the bathroom wall, I tried to focus on breathing in slowly. Once I could catch my breath, I took out the razor that I called my friend. Swiping it against a scar on my wrist, I made another cut to mark the eventual end of my existence.

*****

After weeks of lying around in bed, I grew tired of the same boring thing. I hated myself and whom I had become. I wanted to sprout my wings, shake off the dirt, and be reborn. I had no way of doing so, though; so instead, I just continued to bury myself under the ground and take a long nap. That would end my misery. I hated being the blind mute, and I hated how I became that way. I was uncomfortable and itchy, and my skin felt small around me. The only time I was truly comfortable was when I was at my mom's house. I was not harassed for information; I was not hit, scolded, or called names. Each time I thought about moving in with her, though, my friends flashed in my mind and how I would be giving them up. The words that Dad and Tonya used to tell me flashed in my mind.

"Don't you see how people look at you weird when you walk in the stores with your mom and her colored husband?"

"Your friends will think it's weird."

"It's not normal to have a mixed family like that…"

Words of hate filled my head about my mom, her husband, and my two little siblings who are half Puerto Rican. It gave me anxiety and made me feel self-conscious, and I began to believe those words and lies. Yet the only time I felt pretty, like myself, or even like I mattered was when I was at my mom's house. I felt like I had a voice, I had fun, and I knew who I could be one day.

*****

Desiring to look and feel appealing once more, I decided against long sleeves and squeezed myself into a nice short-sleeve shirt that showed off my curves. It made me feel good inside that I could possibly be attractive in some way. I knew that this feeling gave me a tiny bit of hope that maybe one day I could be attractive and get Brandon out of my head.

My mother walked into the bedroom and gasped at what she saw. She grabbed my arm and asked what they were. "The dog scratched me," I fibbed, hoping that she bought my story. She walked out of the bedroom. I chewed on my nails, my nerves beginning to grow in the pit of my stomach. I was afraid she would say something to my dad and Tonya. They would be the biggest problems, and I did not want them to know.

An hour later, Tonya pulled up with my other three siblings in the car with her. "My children" is what she called them. "Jeff is in the hospital," she said to my mom. I felt like I disappointed everyone; and now that my dad was in the hospital, I knew that the news of my cutting was not going to be taken well. My mother told Tonya and then lifted my arm from my side to show her. Tonya gasped and covered her mouth. The next thing I know, I am being bombarded with questions of why I would do such a thing. I did not know how to feel or what to say. All of a sudden, these people cared about my well-being. I felt like I had gone from being invisible for months to having a spotlight thrust on me in only a matter of seconds.

"I don't know," I mumbled. It was the best excuse I could come up with.

"How could you not know why you are hurting yourself?" Tonya was exasperated. I could tell she was shocked, as well as a little angry with me. She always had a particular tone when she was angry, and I hated hearing it.

My mom and Tonya spoke about my behavior for the past few months. Tonya mentioned how I was always in my room and kept to myself. My mom, on the other hand, did not experience that when I was at her house. Instead, she mentioned how I was always with the kids having fun. I always felt more comfortable at my mom's. I had fun with Cierra and our little brother, Alex. The two little girls, Julissa and Jalena, always liked when I came over too. I had more fun playing with them than when I interacted with Hali, Brianna, and Jeffrey. There were times I would get along with them, but it would always end in a way wherein I become the odd one out.

I said goodbye to my siblings, and I turned to my mom and did the same. She pulled me into a hug and said, "I love you." The gesture felt weird and uncomfortable. I hated the attention and no longer wanted it on me. I hated myself for not being more careful about my scars. Wishing I could take my previous actions back, I climbed into the back of Tonya's black Durango, and we headed to the hospital.

The way to the hospital was mostly quiet. I felt ashamed, depressed, judged, and like I wanted to wiggle out of my skin. Keeping my gaze on the passing trees, buildings, and occasionally, the sky, I avoided anyone in the car who tried to start a conversation with me or looked at me. I could feel the pain building inside of me. I wanted my friend to help take away the pain. But now that they knew, I knew that I would no longer be able to taste the sweet relief my friend, the razor, gave me for even a second.

Finally, Tonya broke the silence. I knew she would; it was only a matter of time. She began her rapid-fire questions. I was made to answer without hesitation, or I knew there would be greater punishment.

"What did you use?"

"How long have you been doing this?"

"Is this because of your mother?"

These were all the questions she asked.

Dad and Tonya hated my mother. That was no secret. I never fully understood why. I only heard how she was [several different curse words] and how she was not a good mother or anything else. Truthfully, as I got older, I realized that neither of my parents were the best of parents…

*****

Shaking off my anxiety, I watched my other siblings hug my father and slip in to the back of the emergency room. I felt the tension build in my heart and my stomach as Tonya leaned over my father. I knew this was the moment when Tonya would tell him about my arm. I knew by the sharp intake of my father's breath and the cold stare that I felt hovering on me that I was in trouble.

My father pulled me closer to him. Hugging me, he asked why I would do such a thing. No words could escape the building sob in my throat. For months, it was as if I had a blockade cutting off my heart from my body; but just as my father hugged me, that dam broke and released the flood building within me.

Although my heart was reconnected with my body, I was not ready to speak of the horrible things that had happened to me a few months back. I was terrified of the consequences of finally telling Dad and Tonya what had happened. Instead of speaking the truth, I kept the true reason a secret. Instead, seeing a psychologist, seeing my grandparents, and sending me away, became the prime topics.

*****

Sitting at my grandparents' dining room table, I cried as I listened to Dad and Tonya showing my grandparents my arm. That shame crept up my inner walls over and over again as I heard Tonya tell all of her family and friends. I felt like a freak show as she told everyone. I understood that it was wrong; but to me, it was the way I released the pain that I was holding on the inside. No one listened to me the first time; and now, still, no one is listening to me. I was only the freak show being talked about and shamed upon because of what I did. The dam had broken inside of me, but things were still not whole or fixed. They were still scattered about on the inside.

Tonya wanted to send me away to rehab. I hated the idea, but my Pop mentioned counseling instead. Dad agreed, and I began counseling right away. I was all right. Nothing worth mentioning. I just felt like I could not talk about anything because I was afraid it would go back to Dad and Tonya. I was terrified that whatever I told her would go right to them, and I didn't want that. Only mentioning things that I had to, I kept my secrets locked inside of me—they were only for me to know.

My counseling sessions continued as weeks went by. We had moved to a different house in a neighborhood with other kids and teens. As a gift, I was ungrounded and told to make better choices.

*****

Startled awake one night, I found myself in my bedroom sweating and afraid. It was eerily quiet. I turned my back toward the metal closet doors that sat hovering over my bed and tried to go back to sleep. Suddenly, there was the sound of something scratching upon metal that broke the silence. Terrified, I played there with my arms across my body, unmoving. The scratching came again. Footsteps sounded across from my bed, where the bedroom door sat ajar. I was terrified. Silently, I began praying. I saw nothing, but I felt nothing. As quickly as it started, the scratching stopped. I continued to pray and asked the Lord to help me fall asleep.

As the next week went by, Hali, Cierra, and Brianna continued to mess around with the Ouija board. I didn't want to even think about the thing. I wanted nothing to do with it anymore as I suspected it was causing things to happen in the middle of the night.

That night, Dad and Tonya went out and had Hali, Brianna, and JJ stay with me. We sat around the computer watching a music video when all of a sudden, a light in the room across from us flicked on.

Hali started to freak out. "The light was off, and it went on!"

"Are you sure?" I asked.

"Yes! It was off!"

Scared, we all ran to the living room and sat there. Hali clutched my left arm, Brianna my right arm, and JJ practically sitting on top of us. Laughing, I tried to brush it off. But then the metal stand that held blankets and rugs fell over to the side in the hallway right in front of us. We freaked out and waited for Dad and Tonya to come home.

*****

My depression was like a sinkhole. I was trying to climb my way out; but each time I went up, I would sink back down into a hole of blackness. I felt like I was suffocating. The past events of what had happened around my closet and that one night also made me very scared. I hated myself and the things that were happening in my home, and I wanted to run away. As a result of us freaking out, one day, our parents enrolled us in a youth group for after-school activities.

Hali and I got onto the school bus and sat in the seat behind the driver. We did not know anyone who went to East Swamp, so we decided to stick together. As kids filed in, I realized that I did recognize some from school. As I watched, I then saw a familiar-looking figure stepping onto the school bus.

"Hello, Samantha," Julia said as she and Shelby sat in the seat behind Hali and me.

"Hey, I didn't know you came here."

"Yes, we come every Wednesday night."

From then on, the bus ride was full of laughter from us. Julia and Shelby explained to Hali and me how the Wednesday youth-group nights worked and told us who each person on the bus was. I was beginning to feel more comfortable and less afraid. I thought maybe that since my best friend came to the youth groups, they wouldn't be all that bad. A sense of peace and relaxation washed over me. Sinking my back into the seat, I enjoyed the ride and what would be the next two hours of my life.

*****

The first two Wednesday nights I attended the youth group, I became accustomed to the schedule and how things worked. First, we would ride the bus to Milford Middle School, where the pastor and the youth group leaders would prep and pray about the night's lesson. During their prep time, the kids attending that night's youth group would be with their cliques, either talking or playing basketball, football, or soccer. After about fifteen minutes of our free time, the leaders would gather us into a large group. Our pastor would begin our lesson; and following the lesson would be a breakout session for small groups, separated by gender and with different leaders. After about a half-hour of our small-group time, the large group would rejoin; and the pastor would end our lesson with some closing words and a prayer.

Each time I went to youth group, I heard a voice calling me. Something was pulling me, but I had no idea what it was. It was almost like a rope being thrown down into my sinkhole trying to lift me out. I just wasn't sure how to grab it.

One night, Tony began to pray. I remember the words coming out like water pouring over my head. Tony asked the Lord to put it on our hearts to ask for forgiveness of our sins and welcome him into our lives. Jesus is our Lord and Savior and will lead us on the path of righteousness. As Tony spoke, I felt as if the water being poured onto my head was filling up my lungs. I felt suffocated, and something inside of me was begging me to be released. As the conclusion of the prayer was coming, I felt almost full of water. I needed to breathe and release the pain that was boiling inside of me.

Tony concluded the prayer by asking those who were not yet saved to submit themselves to Jesus Christ—to believe in his sacrifice on the cross to pay for our sins. As he did so, I felt something in my heart growing warmer with each word. The dam building inside of me burst open, and I submitted myself to the Lord. I asked him to forgive me of my sins. I asked him to take care of me, giving me peace and taking my scars. I was tired of hiding and submerging myself in water. As I asked for Jesus's forgiveness and submitted myself to him, I felt as if the flood inside my body was gone. I felt the peace that I have been longing to feel, and the pain inside of me was released. I could finally breathe without a strike of pain in my heart or water in my lungs. I was free.

*****

Each passing week, I made sure that I was at youth group. I wanted to seek Jesus and allow my mind to expand on the meaning of Christianity. Each time I attended on Wednesday nights, my passion and knowledge grew. I became so pumped up that I only ever wanted Wednesdays to come. In addition to growing closer to Jesus, I also grew closer to Julia. She became my best friend whom I spoke everything to. I could relate to her about Christianity, knowing that she believed in the same thing I did; and that was very comforting to me.

Over the next few months, I began praying every day, multiple times during the day. Sometimes it was about my family and how much I grew frustrated with them; and other times, it would be for selfish reasons, such as wanting to run into Brandon. I did not know why, but I felt as if I needed closure from what had happened to me; and in my mind, the only way to gain closure was to see him again.

Each time my friends and I would go to the movie theater, I would hope and pray that it was in that same theater that he molested me in. In my heart, I needed to see the place that it happened in. I needed to know that the place in which it occurred had a meaning to me and that, that meaning was no longer a painful means to destroy me. In my head, it was pure logic. However, in Julia's head, I was holding on to the past.

"You need to learn the lesson God is teaching you to overcome what he did to you," Julia said to me one day.

I had no idea what she meant. I thought I could coax the answer out of her by asking a million questions and seeing if I was right, but that did not work. She flipped to a section in the Bible and read to me out loud, "'Bless those who curse you, pray for those who mistreat you'" (Luke 6:28 NIV).

From that point on, I was determined to let go of what had happened to me. I had to pray to the Lord for Brandon and forgive him of all the pain that he had caused me. I needed to forgive him and create a new life for myself. One in which God exists. One that involved me giving up my life to serve my Lord.

*****

Riding on the bus with my friends, we laughed and grew excited as we got closer and closer to Long Beach Island, where the Harvey

Cedars Retreat was located. I was so excited for this camp. My friends spoke about it very highly, and I wanted to experience the richness and the feeling of God without the surrounding world of temptation, technology, and my family.

The first couple days, I would slump into bed thinking of how happy I was to receive such a wonderful opportunity. There were tons of kids around my age all over, from many different churches. Together we ate breakfast, lunch, and dinner; we worshipped in the morning and in the evening; we played sports, went swimming, went to the beach; and we did so many more things. At night, the thing I loved the most was sitting on the dock with my feet in the water.

As I stood on the beach each day, I watched the waves drift in and out, taking speckles of sand with it. I felt God's presence, and I felt him calling me toward him. It was as if each wave that crashed onto the beach was him reaching for me then trying to pull me into him as the waves went back out. I wanted to go. I felt him; and I wanted to obey, to follow, and to grow.

Throughout my short life, I have learned one *very* important thing: God always prevails. That night, I tried to get our leader, Bethany, alone in the room; however Hali did not want to leave me, Julia, Belinda, or Shelby. She was beginning to make some new friends but was not yet comfortable with any of them. I tried to tell Bethany that I was not ready to talk with her in the room when Hali was there. I was fine talking in front of Julia, Belinda, and Shelby because they already knew what I had gone through.

Standing on the deck that hung over the bottom portion of the building, I stood with Bethany, our leader, as well as some other leaders like Wendy and Megan. Together we spoke about my speaking with someone to come clean of my past sins and get a fresh start in my faith. However, Hali didn't want to leave my side.

I was beginning to feel anxious. I felt like God was putting it on my heart to talk to someone about what had happened to me. I wanted to talk. It was like this overwhelming feeling as if a bulge was stuck in my throat and needed to come out. I was choking on it, and I needed to cough it up.

Just then, some of the other girls leaned out of their door. "Hali, do you want to have a shaving party with us?" one of them said.

Hali immediately got her razor and went over to the other room, where the other girls were waiting for her. God had taken control of the situation and allowed for Hali to be taken to a different room. I was very thankful and thanked God for his miracle. After watching Hali go into the room next door, the leaders beamed at one another.

"God works miracles," exclaimed Wendy.

*****

I felt dread as we rode the bus home after the long incredible week. I was renewed, whole, and happier than I had been in a long time. I no longer felt like what had happened to me held me back. I felt God on my side; and I knew as a Christian, I was forgiven of my sins. I dreaded going home, though. I didn't want to be around the temptation that surrounded my family house. I didn't want to be around the hateful words, the lies, and the sinful nature. I hated being told not to lie but then told to lie for Dad and Tonya when it came to certain things. It was a contradiction, and I felt that I was destined to fail either way you looked at it.

Trying to play it safe and remain out of trouble, I decided to try and continue learning and growing in my relationship with God by listening to my new CD of the New Testament. I was terrified of returning to a place where I no longer had God. I felt free and whole, and I didn't want to go back to those feelings of depression. It was as if I needed God just like I needed air.

15 Years Old

And the Holy Spirit helps us in our weakness.
For example, we don't know what God wants us
to pray for, but the Holy Spirit prays for us in
groanings that cannot be expressed in words.
—Romans 8:26 NLT

We do not know what to pray for when
we are in moments of weakness. The Holy
Spirit was given to us as a gift from our
Lord God to express what is right, wrong
and to help us communicate to the Lord
our God. Next time you are in a moment
of weakness, take this passage to heart. God
knows what we want and what we need.
—The Daily Bible Devotion App

School finally returned to session, and I was saddened that the summer was over. I am the happiest I have ever been since I devoted my life to God. Trying to do the best I can do, I continued to read the Bible each night as well as pray daily. My parents began to notice the change in me and began making comments on how I seemed lighter. I began to share with them about how I came to be lighter; but as I was speaking, I felt my headaches come back from when I was first diagnosed. Not worrying, I pushed the pain aside and prayed for them instead.

One day, as I walked from the freshman center toward the high school, where my bus was normally parked, I ran into an old friend from middle school.

"Hi, Angela! How are you?"

Hugging me, she responded, "Good, Sammy. How are you doing?"

"Good."

Angela took out a cigarette and showed it to me. "Do you want one?"

"No thanks."

"Are you sure? I have a friend who can give you a whole pack for five bucks."

"No thanks."

As we walked together toward my bus, she told me how smoking calmed her down from her stressors. As my headaches continued to worsen, they became a stressor to me. I contemplated trying it to see if it would help. Thinking through the process, I knew that all of my parents were smokers; Dad, Tonya, and my mom all smoked. I knew Tonya would sit on the couch and constantly light a cigarette every half-hour to forty-five minutes. I thought, *Maybe I should give it a try...*

Standing in the kitchen that night, I saw the carton of cigarettes. *Maybe I could just try one to see if it works.* I looked around to make sure that no one was looking. I slipped my hand into the carton lying on the counter, stole a pack, and ran up to my room. I hid it inside my sweatshirt sleeve and placed it in my backpack, where I knew no one would find it. I would wait for my mom's weekend, when I knew I would not be watched as often as when I am at home.

*****

Sitting on the tiled floor of the upstairs bathroom, I took my mom's lighter, which I had stolen, out of my pocket. Holding the sliver of plastic in my hand made me feel power over my own life. I knew what I was doing was not good. In fact, I knew it was unhealthy and not what God wanted for me. Instead of stopping myself, though, I rolled the piece of metal and clicked the button. A small orange glow illuminated the tiny space in the bathroom. Holding the cigarette in my mouth as I had seen my parents do many times, I held the flame to the tip of the cigarette. As I inhaled, smoke filled my lungs. All of a sudden, I felt dizzy, and a wave of coughs and nausea hit me.

Repeating the process several times, I began to get over the sensation when first inhaling the smoke. Then I heard a jiggling of the knob of the bathroom door. I quickly threw the cigarette down the toilet and flushed it; then, I closed the lid and made it look like I was doing nothing. But I was too slow. The bathroom door burst open, and my mom saw me throw the cigarette into the toilet. Then I looked over and saw the pack sitting out on the sink. I was busted, and I knew that I would have to face the repercussions.

Of course, I should have seen this coming. Immediately, she called my father, and I knew I was in deep trouble then. I suddenly regretted the actions I had taken and dreaded the moment when Tonya would come to get me. Tonya was always the one to pick me up and drop me off. Sometimes it made me feel that Dad just pawned me off to her, as if he didn't want to deal with me.

I dreaded her response and her actions more than his. She was always cold and bitter to me when things like this happened. She made a point to share with everyone what I did wrong, how long I was grounded, and what the stipulations of my grounding were. When it came to Hali, on the other hand, no one heard about her groundings. It was an ongoing war. If I got in trouble, Dad would yell and bring Hali into the mess. If Hali got in trouble, Tonya would do the same to me.

To my surprise, when the Durango pulled up in front of Mom's house, both Dad and Tonya got out of the car. It was worse than I thought. If both of them came with no kids in sight, I knew I was destined to be grounded once more. Words filtered in and out of my head as they scolded me. I began to build the walls back up that I once had before. It wasn't that I didn't care what they said. I just always felt insignificant and belittled, and I just wasn't ready for that familiar feeling of sadness and depression to creep back into my heart.

"You stole the pack from us...grounded..."

It was nothing I hadn't heard before. After the scolding, the question I was waiting for came.

"Why'd you do it?"

"Stress," I responded.

"If it's relieving your stress, you must have been smoking for a while."

"No, I hadn't. I just started."

"There are several cigarettes missing in this pack."

Internally sighing, I fell into old habits and just let them scream, yell, and make up their own conclusions about how long and how often I was smoking. In reality, I only smoked one day. I tried several different cigarettes, but it was only one day. It was no use saying anything though because each time I did, I was called a liar, accused of something that was not true; then I'd be in worse trouble than where I started.

*****

As my grounding sentence continued, so did the onslaught of my headaches. They grew increasingly worse, occurring several times a day instead of just once a day. My grades began to slip, and I began to worry. Speaking to my parents about my headaches, they just thought I was using my vision and headaches as an excuse to butter them up since I was grounded. Although I was grounded due to something I should not have done, it was not my intention to use my disability against my parents.

While sitting on the couch in the living room at my mom's house, I looked to the right toward where Cierra was. She was getting a drink out of the fridge. As she continued to talk about our cousin David coming over, I saw a man standing in the doorway that led to the dining room. He was wearing completely white. He shone brighter than the walls of the dining room, and I was in awe. I looked back at Cierra, wanting to point him out to her. However, when my eyes returned to where he was, he was gone.

After a while, we headed upstairs and sat knee to knee. Suddenly, I saw white legs next to me. At the same exact time, Cierra saw a hand touch me as I felt it on my knee. There was no fear, anxiety, or even coldness. Later, Julia showed me where in the bible it says, "And there appeared an angel from Heaven, strengthening him" (Heb. 13:2 NIV).

Weeks later, my headaches had gotten worse. I was going to the nurse's office every day for them, and my grades began slipping again. Finally, after seeing how often I was going to the nurse's office, they scheduled an MRI to check on the tumor that had been stable for almost three years.

Following Dad and Mom into a well-furnished though unfamiliar room, I felt my nerves begin to vibrate. All of a sudden, I had a dry mouth and was no longer comfortable in my own skin. It was ironic. The room around me was designed to make patients and families comfortable, but I was only filled with dread and fear. As I walked in through the doorway, a dark long oak desk stood in front a white wall with posters I could not read. In front of the desk were two overstuffed chairs. Facing it, behind the desk was another overstuffed chair, and along the wall to the right of the desk was a long black couch. I went for the couch, allowing my parents to sit in the stuffy chairs. I wanted nothing to do with the desk.

I sat on the couch, bouncing my legs while waiting for the doctor to come in. A tall man wearing scrubs and a white coat came in and sat behind the desk. As he did so, he pulled out a white folder. After introducing himself as Dr. Sutton, he began shuffling through the papers and making small talk with my parents. This only made me grow more anxious. Fireworks crackled and spun in my stomach, waiting to burst open and yell, "SURPRISE!"

"Samantha will need surgery to remove the tumor that started growing… wrapped around her optic nerve…major surgery…ten percent chance of this surgery coming out successful without any side effects…" The fireworks exploded. They were going off as if someone was lighting them one by one in a line and not waiting until one was done. Together they crackled, burst, and flew round, destroying everything in their path. My father took me by the hand, walked me out of the office, and handed me his cell phone with my Pop-Pop on the line. "Here talk to Pop-Pop," he said.

Dad disappeared back into the room to continue talking with the doctor. I sat with the phone to my ear. I heard my Pop-Pop's voice, but crying, I barely registered what was being said or even what I said. I envisioned this new girl in front of me. One without problems. One who was tall, thin, beautiful, and had no issues seeing. I wanted to be her. I wanted to shed my skin and embrace a new being altogether. I didn't want to lose my eyesight completely, have to relearn everything as if I was a baby, or die on the table. All those were my options with only a 10 percent chance of coming out completely fine. The odds were not in my favor, and I was terrified.

*****

The next week, Dad and Tonya threw me a sweet 15th. They thought that since I had a low survival chance, I should have a big party. Laughing and carrying on, I was able to forget the bad outcome I was destined to face. My friends and I exploded a potato all over the kitchen, dressed up in outfits, and had a race to eat ice cream cake with no hands! I looked all around at my many friends. I knew that when I died, I would die happy. I was finally okay with leaving this world.

The next day, I spoke with Hali about my impending death. We spoke about the good times we had together when we were young. Being girls and so young, we would watch Mary Kate and Ashley movies pretending we were the twins. After laughing at our young and childish games, Hali's face and tone of voice grew serious.

"You know, Dad thinks it is his fault for what you are going through, right?"

Looking at her, I blinked and asked, "What?"

"Dad thinks you losing your eyesight and now going through surgery is his fault because of all the bad things he has done in his life."

"How do you know? Did he tell you?"

"No, I overheard him and Mom talking in the kitchen."

After pondering on what Hali had told me, I ultimately decided that no, it was not the reason I was going through this misfortune. There had to be another reason. Lying in bed that night, I prayed to God that he would reveal why I was going through this hardship. It was causing so much grief in our family. I knew God had a reason even if I did not know it; and even if he didn't have a reason, he would bring good out of the bad.

*****

Sitting before a computer at school, I wrote a poem for my dad. As I began to write, all the memories poured out of me like flowing water. I wrote them down and continued my poem, incorporating them into it. I was worried that if I did die, my dad would snap. He had a large anger issue, and I wanted him to be okay. I accepted my death, so I wanted to make sure he would too.

> Dad,
> Remember when I sat on the motorcycle with you as a child.
> Remember when I was scared to sit in the back, but loved riding in the front.
> Remember when you took me on the wave runner, you hurt your hand but you didn't care as long as I was having fun.
> Remember our father daughter dance in girls scouts so long ago.
> Remember how you call me your hamster.
> Remember how you love me so much you would do anything for me.
> Now it is my turn to do something for you. Love and take care of Tonya and the kids. Do not get angry or sad that I am gone. I am in a better place now full of happiness and light. I love you and will always be happy for all the fun things we did. Remember to love and to keep going. Even if I am gone.
>
> Love,
> Sam

I gave the poem to Julia and asked her to give it to my father about halfway through the surgery. I was not sure when I would pass, but I really thought it was my time to go to heaven with the Lord. I was ready, and I just wanted to make sure that my dad would have a piece of me.

Julia, Belinda, and I laughed, danced, and ate licorice until about ten o'clock the night before my surgery. They decided to sleep over so we could all pile into the car together instead of roaming around Quakertown to pick everyone up. I had a blast on my last night. As we lay down to sleep, tears slid down my face. I was happy, and knowing that I was happy with my friends gave me confidence that I lived a happy life.

*****

Poking and prodding disturbed my sleepless night. Rolling over, I saw my dad. I knew it was time to get up. After waking up Julia and Belinda, we got ready and piled into my dad's large truck. Uncle Joe sat in the passenger seat as all three of us girls sat in the back singing along to songs on the radio. Meeting us there were my mom, grandparents, Nanny, pastor, as well as two girls from youth group.

Once I was checked in, we all gathered in the corner of the waiting area. I spoke with Julia and Belinda to try and calm my nerves down; but as I saw more and more nurses coming in and going out of the big blue doors, I grew increasingly more nervous. My family sat around me whispering to one another. Pastor Dave Kratz and the other girls prayed for me before I was taken back, and I could not help but to wonder if this was truly my time to leave this world.

"Samantha Goshow," a voice called out from across the room. At once, my family rose to their feet, giving me hugs. Cierra, Julia, and Belinda were first. Then each of my grandparents.

"Don't worry. I will be right back. They are only doing height and weight." I tried to comfort Cierra as she clung to me and cried.

"No, you're not, Sam. This is it." My mom's voice rang in my head.

Suddenly, my world shifted, and I knew that this was it. I would no longer see innocent, pure Cierra playing with her little pet shop. I would no longer experience happiness and joy when I hung out with my friends, and I no longer would be able to see my parents.

As I passed through the big blue doors, my nerves began to explode. Every inch of my body wanted to turn and run the other way. I didn't want to be there. I wanted to be out in the sun, enjoying my time with my friends. I felt like there was so much I could do with my life. Although I accepted my eventual death, I realized that there was so much more I wanted to do.

I followed a nurse into a small sectioned-off area with a counter, cabinets, and bed. She gave me clothes to change into, along with a cup for me to use in the bathroom. My hands fumbled with my shirt, bra, and pants. I hated knowing where I was going and wished it was over. Tears started to burst through my walls of solitude, escaping and beginning to pour. *This is it. My life as I knew it is over.* After performing the tasks appointed to me, I slipped out of the bathroom. As I followed the nurse once again, she led me back to my little spot, where Mom and Dad sat waiting for me.

Over the next hour, doctors came in and out to check my vitals and make sure that I was healthy. I could no longer take it. My anxiety built up, and the dam broke. I wanted to escape and begged my parents to leave. I was no longer a fifteen-year-old girl but an eight-year-old child. My outward calmness and collectiveness shattered, and my former childhood years burst forward. I cried and kept saying, "No, I want to leave!" No matter what my parents said or did, it did not calm me down.

A nurse came in and poured red liquid into a small plastic cup. Giving it to me, she said, "Here, drink. It will help you calm down." I took the cup from the nurse and lifted it to my nose. It smelled a lot like feces. I wrinkled my nose and held the cup away from my nose. The nurse looked at me and said, "Yes, I know it is bad." Then she gave me another small cup with a tiny bit of water. She then said, "Here. I cannot give you much, but hopefully this will help." I lifted the sour red liquid to my lips, chugged the substance, and then quickly slurped the little bit of water I had. Gagging, I noted that the water did nothing to help with the gross medication. I sat back in the bed and tried to relax.

*****

My ears picked up words, but I couldn't understand them. Slowly opening my eyes, I saw fingers in front of me. My father spoke again, "How many fingers am I holding up?"

"Two," I said. The words out of my lips were muffled. Then I fell back into a deep slumber. I felt like a brand-new person. A bird with wings spread open, soaring high above the clouds. I felt peace, joy, and the light flowing through my body. As I soared, I felt my wings being tucked back as the haze started to clear from my fuzzy brain. Opening my crusty swollen eyes once more, I looked around. Julia, Belinda, and Cierra were singing our best friends song. It made me smile knowing that I had them by my side.

"Sam, look what Julia and Belinda did for you."

I knew that voice. Looking around, I saw my mom handing me a braided piece of hair tied with a ribbon. Looking closely, I saw three different strands of hair: my light-blond hair, Belinda's brown hair, and Julia's darker-blond hair. Together they were braided in a strand that became one. My eyes peered around the room. Cierra, Julia, and Belinda stood to one side of my bed as Dad, Mom, and Tonya stood on the other side of the room. I was happy to see everyone. As I looked around, I saw the edges become blurry, and I fell back into a foggy haze.

*****

Opening my heavily glued eyes, I peered around in the dark room. The lights were dimmed. The only indication of life was from the slow beeping noise coming from my monitor attached to my arm and chest. Securing my blanket and nightgown around me, I slowly started to sit up.

"You're finally awake." I knew that voice. Looking to my left, I saw my father sitting there watching me. I saw the laptop open and shining brightly against the dimly lit room. Turning to the other side, I noticed a nurse getting ready to check my vitals.

"Can you count my fingers?" she asked. So I did. She patted me on the shoulder and proceeded with asking me what my name was and if I knew where I was; then she continued to check my vitals. The doctor came into my room a couple minutes after the nurse paged for him. Shining a light into both of my eyes, he reviewed my pupil dilation and my optic nerves. Afterward, he asked me to count his fingers. I did as he asked, and then he smiled. "Looks like you overcame all the odds against you."

The doctor stepped to the side, where the nurses' station was; and I overheard him talking to the nurse there about monitoring my recovery. I had a three-month recovery ahead of me. It didn't make sense to me because I felt fine, besides the constant ache on the side of my head. I remembered that he had to cut into my head, so I slowly raised a hand to the left side of my head.

Carefully tracing where they shaved my head, I felt the stitches from the top of my forehead all the way down to my ear. I felt the stitches near my ear and realized that they had to cut around my ear. There were stitches leading to my ear then to the front of my ear. *I wonder if they took my ear off*...I pulled my finger away from my ear and noticed that blood painted the tip of my finger. I asked to wash it off, and the nurse just wiped it away with a sanitary wipe. After lying back in my bed, I lolled back into oblivion.

The next morning, I woke with my stomach bursting with pain. I was hungry. I couldn't remember the last time I ate. Sucking on a popsicle, I began to taste a metallic substance in my mouth. I knew I was going to throw up. Bending over, I began to dry heave. The nurse stood and held a pan under my mouth. Nothing came up, but just the action was terrifying. Resting back, I looked over at my dad. He sat beside me on the chair.

"You know it isn't your fault, right?" I told him. It was not a question but, rather, a statement. I knew it wasn't his fault, what I had. I knew that God works in mysterious ways and that he has a plan for me.

He looked at me, shocked. "How did you know I thought it was my fault?"

"I overheard you talking to Tonya," I lied. I did not want to tell him Hali was the one who overheard what he had said. "I know God has a plan for me. Things happen for a reason. They always do."

Eating the rest of my popsicle, I felt better in a sense. I felt closer to my father and closer to God; and I felt like a new person, regardless of my broken skull.

The next day, I was eating solids again, and the doctor was impressed. He ordered that the steroids and catheters be taken out. Ecstatic, I was happy to know that I would be released from the treacherous bed that held me captive. Right after I was released from my bed, I began to try and walk. I knew Julia and Belinda were coming to visit me soon, and I wanted to be able to show them how much I had improved. Against the nurses' better judgment, I was up and walking around the hallways. Since I was in the intensive care unit, I was not allowed to leave the floor. When I wanted to go for a walk, I had to have someone with me at all times.

When Julia and Belinda came to visit, we were up and dancing in the hallways in celebration of my fast recovery. I did not dance for long, though, because my head still pounded with the excruciating vibration of our celebration. After witnessing our celebration dance, the nurse scolded me. My skull was not completely healed, so I needed to be careful. I did not care, though, because I had defeated the odds against me and was healing faster than expected.

The day after my celebration with my friends, the doctor came into the room to examine me. He shone a light into my eyes, checked each of my reflexes, and examined my head for any abnormalities. After receiving a green light from the doctor, he said that I could go home. I was so ecstatic that I leaped from the bed (slowly) and smiled as much as I could without my head hurting too much.

Before leaving, the doctor instructed that I was not to climb up the stairs or go back to school quite yet. I would have to be homeschooled for a little while. He wanted to make sure that I would have plenty of time to heal and not harm the area where he made an incision. I was bummed that I could not yet return to school. I wanted so badly to go back to normalcy that it hurt a little inside that I was not permitted to return yet. After receiving all the instructions and signing all the papers, I was finally ready to be set free.

After enduring a month of homeschooling, I was happy to walk back into school, where all my friends were. Going through the motions, I went to each of my classes. I was happy to see my teachers, and I was happy to be alive. I truly did not believe that I would make it. As I sat in my normal classrooms, I felt thankful to God and happy that I faced the darkness and overcame it.

*****

A group project was presented only a few weeks after returning to school. My blood raced with a new challenge, and I was excited to begin diving back into school life. The project involved making a song about different math equations and how to solve a problem using those equations. Together my group and I chose a rap song and created the lyrics to match the rhythm.

After an hour of working on our project, the late buses arrived, and we decided to put our project on hold. I followed Ryan, someone from my group, and sat in the seat in front of him. It was the first time I had ever taken the late bus. I was a little nervous because I didn't actually know if it was the right one. Ryan had told me I would be fine; but these days, I was nervous about everything when I had to read something and depend on another person to guide me. As I sat in the sticky blue seat, I watched another boy climb onto the bus.

"That's Robert, my older brother," Ryan informed me.

Robert was tall and thin. Glasses with thick lenses framed his face. He had curly thick blond hair covering his head. He almost looked grumpy. His hair was a mess of blond curls, giving it an almost fro-like appearance. Wearing blue jeans and an Adidas sweatshirt, he walked down the aisle and sat down. I then looked away and rode the bus in silence.

The next few days were filled with activity: filming, creating a poster board, and rapping to some music, all for our silly math project. Since we were using Ryan's family camera, we had to share with

Robert's group as well. This time, we all worked closely together, sharing the camera and giving the other group suggestions.

As I climbed the stairs onto the late bus, Robert got on after me and sat behind me instead of away from me. Chewing on his licorice, he offered me one. I replied, "No thanks," and kept watch as the bus drove through different parts of the town. Throughout the ride, he talked to me about everything and nothing. Smiling, I nodded along and replied when necessary. I thought he was weird but in a good way. He did not fit into my taste in guys, but he was cute in a nerdy kind of way.

As we got off the bus and into our joining neighborhoods, Robert turned to me. "Can I have your number," he asked. Seeing his hopeful smile, I relented and gave it to him. I wasn't sure why I did; I just knew that I couldn't break someone's effort knowing that they were trying to be kind to me. Walking away, I was unsure of what was to come.

*****

My phone ringing interrupted my thoughts one afternoon. Instead of looking at the screen to see whose picture was on the screen, I answered without looking.

"Hey, Sam. It's Robert."

"Hi. What's up?"

"Just going for a walk."

"Cool."

"Well, I am walking around your neighborhood. Do you want to hang out?"

After thinking about it, I didn't really want to; but against my better judgment, I said yes anyway. Walking outside my door, I spotted Robert standing near our property looking unsure as to how close he should come. He was wearing blue jeans and another Adidas sweatshirt, which was gray (instead of the usual blue). For about an hour, we stood out on the front of my house talking about nothing. Finally, it was time to eat, so we said our goodbyes.

For a couple days, we did the same thing. I would see him at school, and we would say hi to each other. A couple times, we lurked out on the front of my house and chatted about everything and nothing. I wasn't sure of how I felt yet about him. I knew I liked that someone was interested in me. Julia, Belinda, and our new friend Amber teased me about it each day we said hi to each other. However, I still had no idea if I liked him as something more than a friend.

Standing in the parking lot one day, we talked again about everything and nothing. All of a sudden, he asked me *the* question.

"Will you go out with me?"

"Sure," I replied.

At the same time, Brianna came out to collect me for dinner. We said goodbye, and I walked inside filled with pride.

*****

While in church one morning, our pastor spoke about the upcoming baptisms and about signing up. Feeling something in my heart, I knew it was God saying, "Hey, you should do this." Delighted to answer the call, I went and got myself a form, and I asked Tonya to help me fill it out. After filling it out, we had the date set, and I felt eager to become baptized for the first time.

As Julia read my words on the paper, my eyes began to tear up. I listened as she read about my disability, surgery, and wanting to begin a new life following Jesus Christ. I wanted the pain from my past to be relinquished to the Lord, and I wanted to give him everything. Toward the end, where I stated I was giving it all to God, Julia too began to tear up. Her voice croaked, and she had to clear her throat. When she finished, I hugged her and turned toward the pastor.

Stepping into the cold pool of water, I stood facing a wall. Next to me stood my pastor.

"Do you believe in Jesus Christ and his sacrifice saving us from our sins?"

"Yes."

"I now baptize you in the name of the Father, Son, and Holy Spirit."

I placed the handkerchief over my mouth and nose, and he placed his hands on my head. One hand was placed on the front of my head and one on the back. My body was submerged into the water and lifted back up above the surface. As my eyes opened, I felt my pain, suffering, and past slip away. I felt like a new person. I felt the Holy Spirit and the strength pouring into me from God. I was renewed.

The next day, I went over to Robert's house to hang out. Together we sat in his basement just making puppy-dog faces at each other. Sitting in between his legs, I put my head on his shoulder. His finger lightly traced around my arms, up and around my chest without touching anything, then back down the other arm. I felt something grow beside me, and I became confused and uncomfortable. I could feel his hand getting closer and closer to my chest; and when he asked if it was okay, instead of saying exactly how I felt, I replied yes.

That night, after returning home, instead of repenting and speaking the truth about how I felt, I ran from God and what he was convicting me for. I knew I was wrong. I just gave my life to God, and I was stealing it back and running from him. I just didn't know how to get out of what I had done. I was reserved. I wanted a way to take it all back, but instead, it became my spiraling point.

*****

The school year ended, and I was invited to Ryan and Robert's two older siblings' graduation. After watching them cross the stage and receiving their diplomas, the family wanted food. Robert didn't want to go with them; so we were dropped off at their house, and we waited for them to get back with the food. I kind of wanted to go with them, but I stayed behind with Robert anyway.

As the car pulled out, Robert took my hand and led me up the stairs. I was shy but also curious as to what was up there. As a girlfriend, I was not allowed upstairs in any of the rooms. As he led me up the stairs and all the way into his room, we lay there on his bed. It wasn't until he started to take his clothes off when I froze with fear.

The last time that this happened, I was with a boy who took advantage of me and my body. Not knowing what to do, I just let his hands trail over me. My arms and limbs became ice, and my nerves began to vibrate with anxiety and fear.

"Just the head" was what I heard from him, but what he wanted did not process in my mind.

Nodding, I replied, "Sure."

When he started to push, I felt pain. "No," I said quickly. "It hurts."

We stopped what we were doing, and we both got dressed and walked down the stairs. Robert walked into the kitchen and got himself a drink while I lay on the couch. I whispered, "Oh, Lord, what have I done? I am supposed to be with you, and yet I almost gave away my virginity tonight." I was scared and knew I needed to talk to him. That night, as I climbed into bed, I vowed that I would speak to him about what almost happened.

The next day, I went over to Robert's to speak to him about what we almost did. Instead of saying what I intentionally came to say, we ended up making out in his basement. His hands became feverish and livelier as we continued to make out passionately. In my conscience, I heard a voice saying, "STOP!" But my body reacted in ways I did not know it could. In a second, his pants were off, and so were mine. Together we fell to the floor and feverishly kissed until the fever was released, and my temple was broken.

16 Years Old

If someone claims, "I know God," but doesn't
obey God's commandments, that person
is a liar and is not living in the truth.
                                    —1 John 2:4 NLT

Having a relationship with Jesus keeps you
grounded. This is a good thing. With a
grounded relationship, there is room to grow.
The truth is spoken, conviction is felt, and
confidence in God grows. When you walk
alone, know our Lord God is with you. Try
opening that door to a relationship back up
by praying to him, reading his word, and
listening to his will. God works in mysterious
ways and always opens his arms to you.
                      —The Daily Bible Devotion App

While sitting in church one day, the pastor announced how they
were gathering teams for several different mission trips. One of
which was to go to Mississippi to help rebuild the homes for those
who were hit by Hurricane Katrina. As he spoke about the damage
and how they needed individuals to devote a week of their time to
this trip, I felt the Holy Spirit rise up within me. A voice whispered
to me that he wanted me to go on this trip. Standing up after service,
I told both Julia and Amber that I was volunteering; then I signed
up immediately.

Lately, each time I felt or heard a whisper from God or the Holy
Spirit, I ignored it because of Robert. I felt the Holy Spirit when I

was with him; however, I also felt something else saying that it was okay to be with Robert. I could not tell the difference between the two anymore. The voices that were mine and God's melted together into one, and I no longer knew what was being said by God.

The night before we left, I said goodbye to Robert, turned off my cell phone, and hid it in my house so that I would not be tempted to bring it with me. I did not want to bring it and become distracted by life instead of serving God. As Robert went home that night, he was sad and annoyed that I was not bringing my phone. He did not want me to go, but I felt in my heart that it was the right thing to do. I missed God, and I wanted him to be proud. I was a Christian, and I was not going to revoke that title because I was dating someone.

The first day was exhilarating. Julia, Amber, and I were assigned with two other girls from our church and another woman from a different church to stain some decks to already-completed houses. The sun shone hot and bright down on our backs. As we continued working for hours, sweat dripped off of us. Chatting about how hot it was, what the weather was like in Mississippi compared to back home, took up most of our day. Robert was on my mind from time to time; but as the hours progressed, he became a single thought from time to time instead of on my mind constantly.

Instead of feeling sorrow that I was away from my boyfriend, I felt happiness to be with my friends. I felt like I could make a difference, and I felt that there was more to what I was supposed to do in life. The feelings were odd and strange. I did not feel this way any other time. I wanted to embrace it, but I felt like it was still out of my reach. The tips of my fingers briefly touched the happiness, the positivity, and the friends that I felt connected to once more; but something kept pulling me away.

*****

The piano played in the background as we all stood and worshipped together after a long day of hard work. The floor opened up to anyone who wanted to share their testimony. As a young man stood, my stomach began to clench with an unfamiliar feeling. As this man spoke about his time in jail for doing drugs, that unfamiliar feeling spread throughout my body demanding to be heard.

Understanding dawned on me as I continued to listen to this man's testimony. The Lord wanted me to tell Julia about what I have done, what I was doing, and all the details of my relationship with Robert. He wanted me to come clean. He wanted me to speak the truth and hear his words. Guilt, anxiety, and doubt plagued my mind. I didn't want to do the thing that he was challenging me to do. Instead, I was ashamed, and that shame made me feel doubtful of what I was hearing. But then, *humility* was the word I heard from the Lord.

"Julia, God wants me to tell you something."

"What?"

"I, uh…I had sex with Robert."

The fear inside me met with a peaceful wave of understanding and comfort. The two that battled within me came to an end with peace and comfort winning out. For some reason, instead of being fearful of being judged, I felt relieved. I felt like all the pain and suffering that I had been going through because of my ultimate sin was destroyed with just my confession alone. Looking up to the sky, I felt God's presence and him watching over us. I knew he was there and intently listening to the conversation. He was guiding us. He wanted me to do more, but I just didn't know what yet.

"Oh, Samantha, why didn't you tell me?"

"I was scared. I knew I did something wrong, and I thought you may judge and scold me."

"No, I knew something was wrong. I just didn't know what it was. What do you think God is telling you to do now?"

Looking up to the sky, I heard what he had wanted me to do; but I didn't know why, and I didn't want to believe what I was hearing. "I have to break up with Robert," I said. Thunder sounded off in the distance, along with the illumination from lightning. I knew God was confirming what I said out loud. In my mind, I asked if one day we could get back together. I knew the answer was no; but on the inside, I thought maybe I was hearing God wrong. My heart broke into so many pieces. I knew it was the right thing to do, but I just didn't want to do it.

"I don't want to break up with him."

"I know. But God always has a plan for us."

Turning to Julia, I confided in her about the relationship problems that Robert and I were having, particularly how I asked to remain abstinent and how he gave me a hard time about my request. There were many other issues that were coming up in our relationship, like how I felt like I was not able to see or talk to my friends anymore. Robert blamed my friends for our problems, but it wasn't them. It was us with the problem.

"It is time to break up with him, Sam. God is calling you back."

I knew Julia was right. I just hated knowing that I had to do it.

*****

Over the next few days, as we worked on various houses, I felt that God had not left my side. Every single time we got into the truck to be taken to our next house, the song "Letter to Me" by Brad Paisley played over and over again on the radio. Each time I heard it, I knew God was telling me something.

It started off with the boy and some things that he had done, proving that it was his current self addressing his teenage self. Then the song went on to talk about heartbreak and how he would move on from this relationship, eventually marry a beautiful girl, and have kids. God is with him, and that heartbreak will heal. This song sang to my heart; and each time it played, I felt God singing it to me.

My heart was set on doing what God wanted me to do. So I took God's hand and planned on breaking it off with Robert. I knew from the song that God would be with me each step of the way. I knew that he had a plan and that eventually I would heal, grow from the experience, and find my person, who would be my one.

*****

As we pulled back onto the church parking lot late at night, I took a deep breath and prepared myself to go home and do the thing that would break me. Julia gave me a hug, and I was on my way. My heart was broken, and I wanted desperately not to do what God was calling me to do.

After greeting my family, I pulled the cell phone out of my hiding spot. I dialed Robert's number and waited for him to answer. After I told him that I was home, he told me that he was already walking to my house. It was nine at night, and I was tired; but he was already on his way, and I needed to break up with him and get it over with.

When he got to the house, he hugged me. "How are you?"

"Good. What did you do all week?"

"Nothing, Sam. I was bored out of my mind."

For the next fifteen minutes, I told him what it was like building and cleaning finished homes and how amazing it was to see the happiness on the faces of the people we helped. He told me how he played video games and went on a lot of walks.

Taking a deep breath, I turned to him and told him how we needed to talk. Spilling my guts all over, I told him what it was like for me in Mississippi. I was free and happy. I felt God with me, and I had a best friend again.

"I knew you were going to say something like this."

"Robert, I don't want to, but I feel like God is saying we should break up."

His face changed from sadness to anger.

From there, our conversation spiraled out of control. Robert got angry, and my stomach got queasy. I hated going through the motions like this, but I knew in my heart that I was doing the right thing. By the end of the conversation, his goal was to become a Christian so that we did not have to break up. It made me happy that he was willing to change for me; but in my heart, I still knew God wanted me to break up with him. Lying in my bed that night, I heard a familiar voice ask me if I trusted him. I replied, "Of course, I do."

*****

A week later, I was in the hospital with Tonya, my grandmother, Robert, Brianna, and JJ. Together we sat in the waiting room, waiting for the results of my recent MRI. It had been eight months after my surgery, and I was due for a checkup. I acknowledged that my headaches came back, as well as God's question of "Do you trust me?" I knew that something was wrong.

"Samantha, how are you?" Dr. Phillips, my oncologist, asked me.

"Doing well. My headaches are back, but otherwise good."

"Well, after reviewing your brain MRI, you have three new tumor growths. One on the left optic nerve, the right optic nerve, and in the middle. Dr. Liu and I believe that you should be treated with radiation therapy to ensure the tumor growths do not progress."

Tonya and my grandmother were disappointed about the recent discovery, but I knew it was coming. God had warned me, and I knew in my heart that this was the thing he had warned me about. My grandmother and Robert took Brianna and JJ down to the McDonald's attached to the hospital while Tonya and I walked across the bridge to get blood work done.

"What do you think?" Tonya asked from across the tight hallway.

I shrugged. "I knew something was wrong."

*****

The next couple of weeks, the only constant in my life was Robert. Despite what God had told me, I chose to believe Robert's words of how he was going to change and try and learn more about God. I traveled to Philadelphia to visit the Pearlman Center quite a few times. The purpose of my first visit was to meet the doctor who would be following my treatments.

"Hi, Samantha. So what we will do is make a mask specifically for you that will be bolted to the table in the radiation room. We will target these three areas"—pointing to my left temple, middle of my forehead, and my right temple—"here, here and here. The radiation will specifically target these three areas to shrink your tumors and hopefully stabilize them."

"Will I get sick or lose any of my hair?"

"Typically with radiation, you do not get sick. You may feel nauseous, but we can prescribe you medication for that. You may see hair loss in those particular areas of your head, but overall, no, you will not have any hair loss."

"What will be her symptoms once the treatment begins?" asked Tonya.

"Nausea, slight hair loss at the particular areas, short-term memory loss, and she may feel exhausted after the treatments."

My treatment started the next week once the molding of my face was complete. The first visit I had was terrifying. I lay on a table, and a doctor bolted my mask to it before leaving the room. Once the room was locked and secured, the machine that hovered above me began to move and emit a green light. The table spun around and stopped three separate times. Each time, the machine targeted the specific area that the doctor had shown me.

The side effects did not kick in until about my second week of treatment. All of a sudden, I became nauseous and tired. I fought it at first because I wanted to go and hang out with my friends. I did not want to be locked in a house with my stepmom while the rest of my siblings went outside and played with their friends. Tonya would ask me to stay inside after my treatments for an hour just in case I felt nauseous or tired, but I fought the overwhelming exhaustion and stayed awake. I didn't want to be that sick kid, but eventually the exhaustion got the best of me.

*****

After my radiation appointment one day, I walked into our living room with a somber mood and sat. Sitting me down, my dad told me that my mom had left my stepfather, and no one knew where she was. I took the story in; but I couldn't tell if this was a joke, a real thing, or if there were lies being told. It was no secret that my mom and dad hated each other, and both of them told lies about the other. However, as we rode in the car to my mom's house, Dad told me about how Cierra was coming to live with us permanently; my brother Alex would live with his dad, Rich; and the girls, Julissa and Jalena, would be living with Miguel, my stepfather.

Walking into the large house, I saw papers thrown about, clothing everywhere, and Cierra's and my room destroyed. It was utter chaos. We were unsure as to what had happened here, and I became angry with my mother. My Nanny was going through papers by the computer. Cierra was gathering her things in her room, and Miguel was sad and angry. I felt terrible and couldn't understand why my mom would do such a thing. Going over some of the music she was listening to, I had a feeling she was becoming unhappy. However, I did not think she would do something like this. She left us, the kids, her house, and her husband for another man she worked with. I didn't know how to feel or what to think. I just knew it was wrong.

*****

Our worlds were turned upside down. I felt overwhelmed with all the emotions and facts that were surrounding me. I was experiencing memory loss, losing hair in the aforementioned targeted areas, and suddenly my mother was gone. The worst part was that Cierra and I had to give up some things that we did not want to give up. Cierra was forced to come live with Dad, Tonya, Hali, Brianna, JJ, and myself. This meant leaving Julissa, Jalena, and Alex behind to their dads. The next challenge was the rest of our family. Living with our dad, we had no idea when we would see other siblings, our cousins, our aunts, and our uncles, with whom we were so close. It was a dramatic change.

Knowing my mother abandoned Cierra, Alex, Julissa, Jelena, and myself hurt. I knew she cheated on her husband and ran off with another man; but at the same time, I did not want to believe the facts. On the outside, I showed everyone that I did not care. I said and did things to impress my father and stepmom. They were always *complaining* about her and telling me that my mother was a bad person. However, on the opposite side, Cierra was taught that my father and Tonya were the bad people. It was never consistent. We always had either of our parents bombarding us with questions about the other, trying to find secrets through us, or comparing Cierra and myself to our mother, which had a bad connotation in our house. It was never fair and never right. This led to depression for both Cierra and myself.

*****

As my treatments continued, I was put on new medications to help me eat and move past the nausea. Inevitably, the steroids made me gain noticeable weight. I was accused of not taking my medication even though I was gaining this weight and called fat and ugly. The constant name-calling was beginning to break my walls, and I started to believe all of it. I hated my appearance, so I started wearing clothes that did not fit me right. I dressed how I felt, and I was called worse names by Hali, Cierra, Tonya, and my father.

Cierra and Hali's bond grew stronger as my own bond with Cierra grew weaker. My rage toward Hali started a fire in my heart that I didn't know how to quench. They began to plot against me. They tried several times to trick me into looking somewhere else so I would not see them steal my money, the total amount of which accumulated over the years. Hali began to steal my clothing as well and always wanted to bash me about something. I had no energy to fight. Besides, even if I did fight, I would be the one in trouble, not Hali or Cierra.

I began to hate Tonya, Hali, and Cierra. My rage boiled over and turned thick with poison. Each time Cierra and Hali did something wrong, it was overlooked. One night, Hali and Cierra stole a pack of cigarettes for a person in our development. When asked about it, they both lied. It wasn't until Dad looked at the carton that he noticed two packs missing. Of course, he confronted them; however, they were not punished. My anger turned red and raw. I was outraged that they did not get in trouble when I did. I hated where I was and hated that I had no way out.

*****

Dialing Robert's number, my phone announced that I was almost out of minutes. I had been asking my dad for a while, but he had been too busy to put more minutes on my phone. Dialing my own number, I pressed 1 and listened to the instructions coming from the automatic service.

"To add money to your account, press 1."

I pressed the button. "Enter in the amount you wish to add."

Pressing 2 and 5, I entered in twenty-five dollars.

At first, I felt guilty. This meant stealing from my dad again, and I knew from my past experience that stealing was not a good idea. Locking that feeling of guilt in a box, I hid it somewhere in my subconscious. I did not want to feel that pain and guilt. I felt as if my dad did not care since all his attention was put on Cierra. Very quickly, Hali learned the truth too. If Cierra asked Dad for anything, the answer would always be yes. Instead of facing the guilt and repenting, I locked my guilt in a box and continued to add minutes on my phone.

*****

While sitting in Robert's house, his mom announced they were going to go to their trailer at the beach for the weekend. Since my radiation had started, we had to give up our vacation plans. I had to give up Harvey Cedars, the youth group beach setup that our youth group went to every summer for a week. I loved going. It was amazing feeling God's presence, and I could really use it right then during my treatments. However, it was not possible.

My heart was broken since I loved that place so much. Harvey Cedars was my home and where I felt God the most. I needed him during this time of need, with my radiation treatments and my mother abandoning me. When I was told that I could not go so I could continue my treatments, I was pain stricken. Tonya gave up her vacation plans with one of our old neighbors. For a week, she was supposed to go and visit her and spend time at the beach, but now Tonya would not be able to do so either. Instead of going on these vacations, most of Tonya and the kids' time would be spent at the Quakertown pool.

I hated going to the pool. By the time I got there, it was about already two o'clock, and I was very tired. The sun hurt my eyes even more, and I hated having to try and find her. Walking into the pool area, none of my siblings were there to meet me. Tonya did not have a cell phone, so I could not call her; and I had no idea where she would sit. Walking around the pool area alone, I kept my head low to protect my eyes. She had not told me where she would be, and my heart was heavy with fear that I would not find her. As I was walking up to the grassy part of the pool area, I heard my name.

"Sam, we're right here!" I heard Hali's voice call out.

Tonya and Hali were sitting less than a foot away from me. I had passed right by her, and she didn't even call out to me. Instead of calling out to me, she assumed I was not looking. Rage and hatred boiled inside of me. I could not say anything, though, for fear that I would be grounded or reprimanded for my actions. I backtracked, pulled over a lounge chair, lay down, and closed my eyes for a little bit.

That night, I went over to Robert's house. It became my safe haven, a home away from home. Even though I knew that God had told me to end it with him, I couldn't because I would lose my safe haven, and I became fearful of losing my way away from the people I lived with. My father had joined a biker club and was starting to go away on trips a lot. I could no longer have my solitude or invite a friend over to my house. I felt as if everyone were out to get me. Hali and Cierra played evil pranks on me, and I felt as if Tonya was mad at me for taking her summer away. There was an underlying tone with her every time I entered the room or asked her for anything. The answer was always *no* if I wanted to do anything. I did not feel comfortable in my own house, and it was starting to eat away at my skin.

I kept thinking to myself that if she wanted to go on her vacation, she could have just gone. It wasn't like she was taking me to my treatments every day anyway. My grandparents were taking me every single day that I had a treatment. Of course, my uncle had taken me once when they could not, or my Nanny had taken me twice to spend time with Cierra and me; but other than those times, my grandparents took me every single day.

Luring my father to Robert's house before he left on his trip, I had his parents ask my dad if I could go with him. I was very afraid that if I asked him, it would be an immediate no. I was afraid he would talk it over with Tonya, and I knew for a fact that she would say no. I just needed to get away from everyone. I needed to be rid of this pain, and I needed to ask my Dad's permission without my stepmom.

"So can Sam come with us? I promise those two will be separated and will be under supervision the whole weekend."

"Please, Dad," I pleaded with him. I knew he was considering the possibility of me going with them, but I knew my chance was stronger and bigger with him hearing it from Robert's parents.

"Okay, let's go get your bags packed. I'll deal with Tonya."

Happiness fluttered throughout my body. I was free for the weekend! I knew my tiredness may be an issue, so Robert's parents reassured my dad that they would take care of me and allow me to get plenty of rest. I would be sleeping in a queen-size bed with their daughter, Samantha, so they knew nothing could happen between us two teenagers. I did not care what the parents were talking about. I was just excited I would get away from this place.

Sitting on the man-made beach, I stared at the lake ahead of me. I felt God's presence, but it was so far away. I needed him to get through this radiation therapy, but he was so far away. I imagined myself reaching out to him but stopped short. I knew I could not reach him. I was there but just barely. I knew God had told me to break up with Robert, but I didn't have the courage to do so. I knew God was telling me to end it, or a long road would await me to be free; but all that mattered to me was where I was in that moment. I was free from my house, where those piranhas waited to devour me. I was free...but not free enough.

Returning home from my weekend getaway was terrifying. I knew my dad wouldn't be home. He had called me, asking for fudge and saying that he would not be home when I returned. I knew the evil dragon inside would be spewing out red-hot fireballs just out of her nostrils alone. Walking past the blue door that separated the world and my prison, I felt the tension in the air. Tonya sat on the couch watching TV. Looking my way, she said nothing.

"Hi, Tonya," I greeted her.

"Hello," she simply said.

I knew she was mad just by the way she was talking; so I retreated upstairs to my bedroom, where I unpacked. Hiding upstairs in my room, I wrote in my journal about my weekend. Once we were all called downstairs for dinner, Tonya had said to me that it was nice for me to get my vacation when they all had to cancel theirs for my radiation treatment. Not replying, I just thought, *You didn't have to.* I would have been willing to stay somewhere else to allow them to get their vacation as well. That night, I felt the tension and stress jump back onto my shoulders. My shoulders twinged with pain. Once again, I thought that I needed to get away from this place.

During the weeks that my father was gone, I tiptoed around Tonya. I hated being around her since she was so unpredictable. I knew she was angry and felt bitter inside. I could feel the pain stabbing at me in waves. I felt as if she took that pain out on me, and I hated all of it. I wanted nothing more than to just become even more invisible so that she could not see me. Instead of speaking, I became a quiet, only talking whenever my friends were around.

I stopped asking her if I could hang out with Julia or Robert because every time I asked, the answer was always no. It pained me that she always said no since Hali was allowed to walk around town with her friends after school. I hated her for locking me in this prison when I did nothing wrong. That is, until the weekend my father returned and Tonya went through their bank statements.

"Jeff, there is money missing in the bank. Where is it all going?"

"I don't know, Tonya. I'm not spending anything I don't tell you about."

I knew where this conversation was headed. I knew that my dad would put the pieces together, and I knew that everything would lead right to me. I got up from the rocking chair and slid into the bathroom. There was silence on the other end when all of a sudden, I heard my father's voice.

"THAT LITTLE BITCH!"

I knew he was talking about me. In the next moment, he was banging on the bathroom door, telling me, "GET OUT NOW!"

"I'm coming!"

"NO. NOW! BEFORE I BREAK THIS DOOR DOWN."

Sliding my pants up, I asked for God to protect me. Immediately after I opened the door, hands grabbed at me and pinned me against the wall. My dad's giant scruffy hands grabbed at my throat. His face hovered only a few inches away from mine, but I heard nothing. I only could see his eyes and his lips moving. His hands grasped tighter and tighter around my throat until I could barely breathe. I was gasping for breath when Tonya spun her head around to see what my father was doing.

"Jeff, you're choking her!"

Sitting me on the rocking chair, my father screamed at me and asked over a hundred times if I took the money to pay for more minutes for my phone. I denied each time they asked me, and soon they got fed up with me and locked me outside the house. I knew they were furious; and the tears kept pouring down my face, along with my anxiety and fear. I knew I had taken the money, and I knew it was the wrong thing to do. I didn't know I would be caught, so I tried to plead with God for him to help me. Looking up to the sky, I saw nothing but blackness. I wanted God to free me from this prison.

For a while, I stuck to my story. I knew I was lying; but I was filled with fear, and that spurred me on. One day, Dad threatened to take a bat and go to Robert's house. Since he was so quick to anger all the time and was a part of the new club, I was terrified that he was speaking the truth. Sneaking on my school computer, I sent a Myspace message to Robert about what my dad threatened to do. But I did not realize that Tonya had snuck up behind me. "What are you doing?" she asked. I was caught.

The next few things happened quickly. First, Dad took my computer and hacked into my account. Next, he was bewildered, rushed me into the truck, and took me to Robert's house. He was buttering up Robert to delete the message without reading it; he was a snake in sheep's skin. I grew even more terrified as he made it sound like it was no big deal. We returned to the truck; and the words *dumb, retarded, stupid, can't think*, and more, penetrated my brain.

After a week of denying that I had used their card to pay for more minutes, I finally admitted the truth. I was already grounded and knew that I could not be grounded any more than I already was. While my dad and I stood in the elevator, I told him the truth.

"Dad, I did use your card to pay for more minutes."

"Why did you lie about it?"

"I was scared."

He then hugged me and told me that it would be okay. He also told me that he would speak to Tonya and that I would only be grounded for two more weeks.

Those two weeks turned into four months. My siblings were no longer allowed to speak to me because I was an "irresponsible, terrible child." It was said that I was a bad influence, so I was going to be treated like so.

The darkness slowly crept back into my mind and my heart. Glancing at razors, I had the urge to use one across my skin again. I remembered how it felt, but I also remembered that I moved past that part of my life. I remembered being addicted to the thoughts of blood spilling over my wrist. Instead of giving into it, I wrote poems about death and darkness. I could no longer talk to Robert or my friends outside of my home, so all I had left was my journal.

I began to hibernate in my room. I had nothing else, so my room looked like a great place to seek solitude. However, Tonya caught on to that and grounded me, keeping me away from my room. I was no longer allowed in it, except to sleep at night. The strings holding my sanity, strength, and calm snapped. I began to weaken in my strength until I saw the CD book of the New Testament that my grandmother had gifted me for Christmas.

I pulled out the binder that held my CDs for my audio version of the Bible. After slipping the first CD into my CD player, I lay on the couch in the backroom of the house. The Book of Matthew began, and my heart was opened. I began to listen to the Bible every day. I was refilled with hope and faith that I had not had in a long time. I was proud of myself that no matter how much I may be a prisoner in my own house, God was with me, and the apostles had gone through so much worse than I was going through.

*****

A knock sounded on the door one day while Hali and I were in the living room. It was a man looking for our parents to repo the car. Tonya hid upstairs in the bathroom and told us to tell the guy that no one was home. As we repeated the lie, he mentioned how one of the children were having brain surgery. "Oh, that's me," I quickly replied. However, that was the wrong thing to do. After he left, I was scolded for commenting and told to "keep my mouth shut." I never knew when to advocate for them.

In our house, we were raised on lies. We were taught to lie at a young age. These lies turned into jokes for our family and their friends; however, when we lied to our parents or said the wrong lie without being prepped, we were scolded. Lying became easy for me. I knew how to lie, what were the best lies, and how to not feel guilty because that was what we were taught. However, as weeks went by and I was continuously scolded about lying to them about the money for the phone, I grew tired of it all. I wanted out of the prison that was full of lies, deceit, and snakes.

My birthday was quickly approaching. I was delighted to imagine turning eighteen in two years and leaving this prison. I felt unsafe between the verbal attacks from my siblings, stepmother, and father (when he was home), as well as from the stress and tension that constantly radiated throughout the house. I didn't care how I would leave, if I was homeless, or how I would feed myself. I just imagined myself away from the house that I was living in, and that gave me a tiny spark of hope in my chest to keep moving forward.

*****

"Sam!" my father shouted for me one day. I walked down the short hallway toward the living room and found Dad, Tonya, and Hali sat on the crusty tan couches.

"Sit please," he instructed.

I sat down on the rocking chair waiting expectantly. I knew I had done nothing wrong; so I suspected that Hali must have done something wrong, and I was dragged into her problems once again. The way our family worked was that each time Hali or I did anything wrong, the other's name was dragged into it. For example, I stole money, so Hali was in trouble for not cleaning her room. Now Hali's grades were slipping, and she got caught doing something inappropriate; so I was mentioned because of how I stole from them. It was unfair, but that was what Dad and Tonya did.

"You're ungrounded," my father said to me.

Just sitting there, I waited as Tonya yelled at him. She was saying that they were two different circumstances and that my punishment should not be lifted. Sitting on the rocking chair, I stared straight ahead at the new giant TV. They claimed it was for me to see because of my eyesight, but I knew it wasn't because they cared. No, it was because they wanted a newer TV. Yes, I could see it, but I was never a TV-watching. kind of person.

By the time Dad and Tonya were done arguing, Tonya was seething, and Hali and I were there just to witness the argument. That was how things went these days. Argument after argument, with the anger taken out on Hali and myself. We were their constant puppets in arguments, most likely because we were not their biological children—Tonya was my stepmom, and Dad was Hali's stepfather. In this case, since my dad was missing half the time, I ended up with a lot of the repercussions.

For the first few days, I decided to lay low. Of course, I told all my friends that my dad said I was ungrounded; but since he was gone again, I decided not to push it. I knew Tonya was unhappy about it, especially since she thought I should have been grounded for longer than the four months that I was. With my birthday coming up, my dad said to think of something to do.

I decided to turn my life around. I had made a commitment to God, and I was not honoring that. Looking up different clubs that I join, I decided to be a peer buddy for one of the special-needs students at school. In addition, I decided to speak to Robert about the "extracurricular activities" that we have been doing. I no longer wanted to do them. But instead of focusing on what I didn't want to do, I made a list of fun things that we could do as a couple that did not involve the inappropriate activities.

*****

Plugging in my headphones, I continued to listen to the Bible even though I was no longer grounded. It was my saving grace. I wanted to continue learning about Jesus and his disciples. The only way I knew to do that was to listen in my youth groups, as well as listening to my Bible. I began to prefer listening to my Bible over spending time with Robert. As I drew, something hit the wall beside me and drew my attention away from the Bible. After pressing pause, I turned to Cierra, the only other person in the room.

"What? What did you throw at me?"

"There's something in the room. Listen."

A sharp, eerie noise sounded from one of the closets by my bed. The doors were metal, and it sounded as if someone was taking long fingernails and dragging them downward over and over again on the metal closet door. Turning off my CD player, I began to get scared. I got up from my bed and walked casually over to Cierra's, and we stared at the closet together. The scraping noise kept going over and over again.

Too scared to move, Cierra and I just sat there. Fear started to collect in both of our stomachs. The only way out of the room was to go past that closet, and that was not something either of us wanted to do. Both scared out of our minds, we tried to talk to it. We figured that if it was making these noises, then maybe it wanted us to talk to it. Suddenly Tonya opened the bedroom door, and we both jumped.

"Do you guys have any laundry that needs to be done? My load is too small," Tonya said.

I got up off of Cierra's bed and went to my closet. The fear still resonated in my stomach; but I thought that since Tonya was still standing right there, it would not do anything to either one of us. After grabbing some clothes and giving them to Tonya, I took my Bible and went downstairs with Cierra on my heels. We silently communicated to each other not to talk about what just happened. We were both terrified and wanted nothing to do with what was back there.

A week later, the incident was forgotten. Instead, I became fixated on the flickering candlelight that was my relationship with Robert. I knew it was only flickering on my end; however, I also knew that I needed to do something about it. I desired a rock in my life though. I needed something solid, something steady; and I thought Robert was that rock. I needed him; and his arms wrapped around me, allowing me to continue living with the large unstable family that I had. There was never a dull moment in our house, and I wanted so badly to leave and forget about this place.

*****

The winter retreat was coming up; and of course, Julia, Amber, Belinda and I were signed up. Just like Harvey Cedars, this was my favorite time of year. I loved going on retreats away from my family and the evil sins that I was born from and raised in. My only fear was that I would hear God once again say that I had to break up with Robert. I knew it was coming. I felt it ever since Mississippi, and I knew that I was running from the fact that I still had to do it.

The retreat, like any other, was fantastic. The schedule was mostly the same each day: breakfast, worship, a half-hour to do devotions, some free time, activity and group time, lunch, free time again, dinner, and then more worship. I simply loved this place. I felt at home, I felt God's presence, and I was with my friends. I never wanted to leave.

Standing on the red carpet, I sang until my lungs gave out. I worshipped God and felt the Holy Spirit stir as I did. I felt it grow with each word that sprung out of my mouth. It was as if a lion was creeping upward out of a long sleep, finally waking. I felt God. I wanted him. I wanted his presence all around me, and I needed him. The need grew larger and more persistent as we transitioned into the next song. Finally, I could see him. I saw his hand reaching out to me, arms open wide; and I heard him calling my name. I tried to run to him, but something was holding me back. I asked him why, but I already knew why. It was Robert. To gain God, I needed to sacrifice Robert. Although I wanted to, it hurt my heart.

Sitting on the couch next to Julia in the girls' part of the cabin, I asked if I could talk to her about what God was telling me to do.

"God wants me to break up with Robert."

"I know. He wanted you to do that when we got back from Mississippi."

"I know, but he said he would work on a relationship with God so I wouldn't have to. I thought if he got closer to God, I wouldn't have to end things between us."

"You can't change someone. Only God can change that person. I know it is hard, and I know it will hurt. But I am here for you, and so is God."

Before we left, there was one more thing that our pastor wanted us to do. Giving each of us a blue index card, our pastor spoke about how Jesus gave his life to forgive us of our sins in our past, present, and future. Each sin that we may commit is already forgiven. When Jesus died, he became the bridge for us to be able to have a relationship with God. Though each of our sins are already forgiven, we also need to forgive ourselves and hand over our burdens to God. As I placed the pen tip on the card, I wrote down my burdens in life, leaving them up to God.

- Lust
- Sex
- Disobeying God's wishes
- Gossiping
- Stealing from Dad and Tonya
- Hating Dad, Tonya and my Mom

After writing our sins and burdens down on the blue index card, the pastor asked us to write in big block letters over all of our sins Jesus's name. After doing so, I folded the piece of paper in half and waited in line to nail my index card to a wooden cross made for this trip. Once everyone was finished, we prayed, and music played for a few minutes in case anyone wanted to kneel at the cross and pray to Jesus.

My heart was beating rapidly. God called out to me. I was being convicted to kneel before the cross and confess my sins. He wanted me close. I desired to go, but I was scared. Mustering up my strength, I stood and walked over to the cross. Kneeling before it, I closed my eyes and prayed. I prayed for forgiveness of my sins—for disobeying his wishes—and asked him for the strength that I needed to break up with Robert. I needed him, and the only way to grow closer to him and fully be with him was to end this part of my life with Robert.

*****

I lifted up the receiver of the large black housephone and dialed Robert's cell phone number. Asking him to meet me halfway, I prayed for strength and began my long walk toward the section where the two developments met. I needed this to be out in the open right away. If I waited or even broke up with him in my house or his, I would chicken out. I needed this to be done in the light. The light was where God was, and I needed God. My overall goal was to end things and silently walk back home, where I could not be disturbed.

"Hey," he said, coming up to me. Then he hugged me and tried to kiss me.

I leaned away from his kiss and replied, "Hi."

"What's wrong?"

"Nothing."

For a few minutes, we walked in silence. Looking up to the sky, I asked for God to give me strength. I did not feel that I could do this. My heart was breaking just standing next to him, but I knew that it had to be done. Giving him the note, I said I was sorry and turned around to walk home. As I turned, so did he.

"I know what this is, and the answer is no."

"I'm sorry. I just need time. I talked with Julia, and I just feel like this is what God wants."

"You know, ever since you went to Mississippi, you have been different. You were going to break up with me then."

"I'm sorry."

I walked away and returned home. The weird part was that even though I felt like I was going to cry, there was nothing but dryness from my eyes. There were no tears—just a broken heart because I felt bad for him. I called Julia on the phone and told her that I did it. I felt like the right thing was done, but I knew it was far from over. I knew something was going to come back and bite me in the end.

The next weekend, Julia came over, and we talked a lot about what God had said to me and what God wanted me to do. I still felt bad for Robert; and every time I saw him walking around in my neighborhood, I felt as if he was a lost puppy. I knew I had forced him to consider God, and I knew that was a mistake. I could see his hatred for God burning like a torch through his eyes and facial features.

Deciding to go for a walk, Julia and I walked through my neighborhood and into the development that connected to ours. As we chatted away, I knew I was beginning to look for him. I thought that if I could see him, I would get peace of mind because I knew he would be okay. As Julia and I rounded the corner of the development, a water bottle came flying at us. Julia ducked, and the water bottle landed and began to roll down the hill. Looking over, I only saw a figure walking toward us. I did not have to see to know who was walking toward us.

"Oh my gosh! He just threw a water bottle at us!"

I stopped, waiting for him to walk up to us.

"Sam, he just threw a water bottle at us! You don't need that jerk in your life!"

"Why did you throw that at us?"

"I didn't. It barely touched you."

"No, Robert. You threw a water bottle at us."

Taking my arm, Julia led me away from him. As we walked into my house, my anger began to boil. I was upset more than anything. However, the water bottle was the last straw. I took the bleach bottle from Julia as we helped Tonya clean the bathroom and nearly threw it at her. I did not mean to. It just happened.

"Woah, Samantha!" Tonya came out of the bathroom and looked at me. "Are you okay?"

As Julia told Tonya what had happened, I retreated to the bedroom. I was so upset and angry. I did not know what to do. I wanted to take him and punch him for that move that he just pulled. As I sat stewing, Julia and Tonya entered the room and sat on my bed.

"I know what you must be going through. You're having problems with Robert, your mom is gone, and you're lost...You threw Windex at Julia."

"No, I didn't."

"Samantha," Julia replied, "you threw the bottle right at me."

I looked down. "I'm sorry. I didn't mean to."

"You need to talk to Robert and forgive your mother. No one is perfect."

"I did forgive my mom." Tears started pooling in my eyes.

"No, you haven't. You are carrying all the weight. You need to give it to God."

Taking her advice into consideration, I called Robert and asked him to meet us at the top of his development, by the mailboxes. While Julia and I sat there waiting for him, my nerves began to bunch up into little balls of fire. I wanted this to be over and my heart to heal. God was my ultimate desire; and in order to gain him, I needed to end Robert and me.

"Here he comes, Sam," Julia alerted me.

Robert walked up to us. I knew he was mad. I could feel his frustration rolling off him in waves. I felt terrible that I had to call off the relationship. I knew he wasn't happy, and I knew my heart ached for him just as much. I just didn't know how to give God what he wanted at the same time as giving Robert what he wanted.

"I know you are mad and upset with me. I know it's not what you want, but I need this break. I need to be able to grow closer to God. I can feel him calling for me, but I cannot grow closer without ending what we have."

I could see the fire growing in Robert's eyes, sucking the oxygen from his bloodstream. His face contorted, and anger poured out of each orifice from his body. Julia tried to help me speak, console, and offer peace; but in the end, he stomped off to go back home. Feeling defeated, Julia and I retreated back to my house. I felt terrible. My heart was heavy, and I couldn't stop thinking about how I hurt him. I knew it was the right thing, but I also felt guilty, like it was the wrong thing.

*****

I sat on my bed, gazing out the window and up to the sky. There were thick white clouds hovering in the sky. The weird part was that I could no longer see clouds, so being able to identify them was shocking to me. As I stared at them, I saw a large figure in the clouds staring and smiling back at me. The figure was wearing white and had brown hair. I noticed that his face was blurry. I felt joy coming off of him and him whispering to my heart, "Write me a book."

A sense of peace came over me. I felt one with God. At peace and whole, I rejoiced in his presence. I would write about my commitment to God and who he was. I would write the story of how I became the person I was going to be and how God was present in my life, guiding me. I wanted to succeed in what he wanted me to do. In order to do that, I needed to write my whole life's story.

Writing on a piece of paper what I had heard God say to me, I folded it up into a little square and slipped it into my father's drawer. My heart was at peace now, and I could feel that the purpose of my life was to write a story of my life and all the hardships I had to overcome during my time as an adolescent. The thing I didn't know was *when* I would begin writing about my vision and the struggles I would overcome. I did not know when God wanted me to start this book, and I did not know *how* he wanted me to write it. All I knew was my purpose was to spread God's Word and share with everyone how God saved me and spread the truth behind his Word.

17 Years Old

And so I tell you, Keep on asking and
you will receive what you ask for, Keep
on seeking and you will find, keep on
knocking and the door will open to you.
—Luke 11:9 NLT

The power of persistent prayer is incredible.
Strength rises up in your voice as you
continuously seek God's voice. Rest assure that
he will always answer through the fulfillment of
your prayer through a strong no or by guiding
your heart in a different direction causing you
to no longer to pray for that specific thing.
Go ahead and pray a specific prayer daily.
—The Daily Bible Devotion App

Only a few short weeks later, I was trapped inside the toxic relationship with Robert again. He constantly was walking around my
neighborhood, around me in school, and consuming each thought
as I tried to stay away. However, after getting knocked on the head
from playing football at gym and going to the hospital, I was in his
clutches again. Looking at me from the hospital bed, he proclaimed
his love for me. I fell for his sad eyes and tried to tell myself that I
could balance him and God.

Caving into his demands once more, I ended up tossing my
morals out the window out of guilt. I did not know at the time that
I was manipulated into having sex. I felt guilty each time I said no

because of the way he would look at me or comment to me. So I gave in.

Walking with Robert from class to class, I realized something detrimental: I was late for my period. Being only sixteen, I couldn't fathom being pregnant. *Dad and Tonya would literally kill me!* Taking Robert aside to speak with him, I told him of my worries.

"I'm late."

"What?"

"I didn't get my period yet!"

Robert looked at me with a dumbfounded expression on his face. I was beginning to panic. If anyone knew the possibility, I would be dead; and this time, I would not just be let off of my grounding because of something Hali did wrong.

Two weeks later, I still didn't get my period, and anxiety began to plague my mind. I needed to break and tell someone. I needed a test. Anxiety, the overwhelming desire to know, and fear, all boiled deep in my belly. I needed to know. Taking my dad's word of how we can come to them for anything without judgment, I cornered him in the kitchen one morning while he was eating cereal.

"Dad, you know how we said we can come to you about anything?"

"Just tell me."

"I didn't get my period this month."

I watched his jaw drop and his spoon drop simultaneously. He stared at me for a couple seconds. Those seconds felt awkward and like it lasted forever. I wasn't sure if I should walk away or stand there while I watch him gawk at me.

"Follow me," he replied. He took me upstairs to where Tonya was and told her what I had said. He laughed. "She's just like her mother!"

I hated those words. Just because I made mistakes, to them, it means I am like my mother…I hated them constantly calling me names and saying that I am like her.

"I knew it! I told you she would be pregnant by the time she turned sixteen. Just like her mother."

Hearing those words did not make me feel any better. I hated thinking she had betted against me because of the mother I was born to. The hatred and anger that I once had for her returned. I decided that she could think what she wanted to think of me. If I truly was pregnant, it means I would no longer be living under this roof. I hated this place and the people in it. I was the lonely sheep of the family because I was not like anyone in the house, and every day I was reminded about how different I was.

"When were you supposed to get your period?" asked Tonya.

"Two weeks ago," I mumbled.

"Does Robert's parents know?"

"No, we were going to tell them after I told you guys."

"Go call Robert. Have him come over. Then together the two of you will go tell his parents."

Robert came over, and together we did the walk of shame back to his house. Without talking, we walked and thought about how his parents would react. I thought maybe his parents would be better because they were more understanding. However, after standing in the kitchen, we remained silent and still like statues as they verbalized their opinions on what we had done. No one could believe what kind of trouble we possibly got ourselves into. I knew that we may not get good reactions. Concerned about my well-being since I was on blood thinners, they asked me to call my doctor to see what they said about being pregnant while on blood thinners.

"Yes, hi. I am on warfarin and may be pregnant. I'm not sure what this could mean."

"Do you actually know if you are pregnant?"

"No, I just missed my period and a little worried."

"Okay, you need to go to the nearest emergency room and get tested. If you are pregnant, then we would need to switch your medication immediately. The medication that you are on could create fatal problems for you and your baby."

Hearing this scared me. I told Robert's parents, and they said we should go. I tried to call Tonya on my aunt's housephone, but no one answered. I made a snap decision, considering the doctor said it was dangerous to be on this medication while pregnant. Then Robert's parents took me to the nearest St. Luke's emergency room.

After being checked into the ER, I waited on the uncomfortable bed hidden behind a curtain. Before I peed into the cup, I heard my phone ring. Upon seeing a picture of my family on the screen, I knew it was my dad. I answered the phone, bracing myself for what he had to say.

"We did not tell you to go to the hospital. Your instructions were to stay at Rob's house until Tonya gets home. Now get your ass home now!" My dad screamed at me from the other end of the line.

Fear grasped my heart and lungs and sucked the oxygen right out of me. I knew it was bad if my dad called instead of Tonya. I knew I was going to be grounded, and I knew that I may get more than just a screaming Dad and Tonya. There would be hell to pay in my house. I got up from the uncomfortable bed and slipped around the curtain. Then I walked back into the waiting room, where Robert and his parents sat waiting for me.

"My dad called. He wants me home now."

Together we silently walked out of the hospital.

"Did you get the results?"

"No, my dad wanted me home now. He is pretty mad, so I'm guessing I am going to be grounded."

Every time I walked into my parents' house, fear overruled my emotions; however, it was fear, anger, hatred, anxiety, and depression that took over my body.

As I entered the cold yellow house, Tonya barely glanced at me as she gave me her directions. "Sit in the chair. Do not speak or get up until your father gets home," she instructed. I sat in the chair, staring straight ahead at the television, not saying a word or seeing anything. My walls began building themselves brick by brick. My heart, my feelings, and my emotions were shoved into a little box buried deep within me.

Each time one of my siblings or someone else would walk through that door, they would say hi to me. Tonya waited to see if I said anything. When I didn't, she would explain that I was in deep trouble and not allowed to talk to anyone. The words "bad influence," "never speak to my children," and "like your mother," rattled around and around in my head. I did not know it then; but I was a troubled teen with not only boy troubles but also *parent* troubles.

My family was divorced. We were all blended, with different children from different fathers and with stepmothers and stepfathers. There were so many of us that it was hard for a parent to give attention to *all* of their children. However, instead of trying to understand the circumstances that we had gotten ourselves into, we were yelled at, screamed at, and punished with the most severe punishments. Hali and I had it the worst. Hali got it from my dad while I got it from Tonya mostly.

I had waited for hours for my dad to return when Hali, Cierra, and my dad walked through the front door with big grins on their faces. "Show Tonya what you got," he told them. Together they lifted their shirts to show tattoos on each of their hips. I was shocked because they were only thirteen and fourteen, and they were okay with letting them get tattoos. However, I kept my mouth shut and continued facing the television. Hali and Cierra excitedly spoke about how they were scared but thrilled at having something that pierced the whole body. The whole time, I sat speechless. I was not permitted to speak, so I did not. Dad turned to Tonya and asked if I sat the whole time. She replied with a yes; then they said nothing else about me until Hali and Cierra went up to our room.

Sitting next to Tonya, my dad finally turned in my direction to begin questioning me. "Why did you go to the hospital?"

"Because I called CHOP to ask them what the medication could do if I am pregnant."

"You waited weeks before telling us. A couple more days could not hurt."

The argument began of why I went to the hospital, what in my right mind would make me listen to a doctor now, and why I didn't call Tonya before going. "I did try," I responded as the tears began to pool in the corners of my eyes.

For hours, it was the same fight over and over again. I should not have gone to the hospital. I should not have left Rob's house. I should not have been a slut and let a boy into my pants...By the end of the one-way yelling match, I was tired and exhausted. By the end, I had new rules and a metaphorical leash and collar.

My new rules were harsh and unfair for such a small crime. You would think that I murdered someone and buried the body out in the back of our house. I was no longer allowed to talk to any of my siblings due to my being a bad influence. I was no longer allowed to be in the same room with my family or sit with them. I had to eat meals by myself after cooking it myself, and this I could only do after the rest of the family ate each night. This was a huge one because I had no idea how to make food since I was never taught. Making things like grilled cheese was fine; but meatloaf, chicken, and other meals, I had no idea how to make. I could only ever get a shower after everyone else, and I had to ask permission first. I was not allowed to do anything, even go to school, without permission.

Tonya woke me up the next morning after only getting two hours of sleep. I had to wait until everyone had left for school when she drove me to her grandparents' house. After dropping me off, she instructed me as well as her grandparents that I was not permitted to sleep under any condition.

Slumping into their couch, I listened to their TV as Grammy watched her shows. *The Price Is Right* came on, and my eyes slowly began to shut. My head became heavy and started to fall off my hand, which propped it up. As I felt my head begin to fall, I stirred myself awake so Grammy couldn't tell Tonya that I slept. Many different times, I had to stir myself awake; and Grammy had told me I could go to sleep, and she wouldn't tell. Mumbling, "No thanks," I continued to fight the sleepiness that was all over my body.

My head began to hurt me, and I wanted nothing more than to fall asleep right where I was. When she finally came to get me, she scolded me some more, telling me how I was burden on her and her family. She added that she didn't want me anywhere near them but especially didn't want me alone with my father. Staying silent, I let her spew fire at me. There was nothing left for me to do than just to sit and take it.

The next day, Dad and Tonya took me to the doctor's for an examination and pregnancy test. As we sat in the waiting room, Tonya warned me, "In one way, you better hope you are pregnant. But in another, you better hope you're not." Tonya's voice rang in my mind. The tears began to build up; but I knew that if I cried, she would be harder on me. Following the nurse back into the room where I would be examined, I waited for the hour of misery to be over.

After the examination, Dad and Tonya both came into the room. I had to suck up my tears and act as if I was not sad. If they even saw a tear, I would be told to knock it off and later on be punished more. Stepping into the room last was the doctor. The doctor said, "Her urine test came back negative for pregnancy, but just in case we will want to take a blood test."

My hopes in ever getting away from the two of them came spiraling down. My depression turned into desperation, and I just wanted the doctor to call me her own child. I did not want to return home with Dad or Tonya. I was afraid for my life, and I was afraid of Rob's whole family. Upon getting into the car, I was told that I was grounded and that Rob's parents would be told by Dad. Once home, Dad and Tonya once again resumed fighting over me. I was now the child who was a slut, stupid, and unwanted. Tonya tried to talk to Dad about sending me to live with my grandparents, but he wouldn't have it. Instead, they argued, argued some more, and then yelled at me.

*****

My life turned and spun dramatically, throwing new and old things at me. Depression slid over my eyes, blocking out the sunlight. Darkness creeped in. Over and over, I prayed to the Lord to save me. I couldn't feel him exactly anymore. I just knew that if I prayed, it would keep that tiny spark of hope lit in my chest.

I began to write poems to try and ease my pain. I didn't want to go back to the slicing and dicing of flesh and dripping of blood. I wanted to release in a healthy way.

A drum beat slowly to an unseen rhythm
The darkness spiraled, twisted, and danced to the
slow rhythm
Dipping in and out of the drum, it begged the
drum to stop
A woman lying in bed helpless to answer the call
Her arm hanging over the edge lifeless but yet
full of life
The drum beat louder
Slowly a light glowed through the window
The light hovered, still as a statue
A hand calling the other one to him at the
window
The drum began to beat a steady rhythm
First slow, but growing in size
Brighter and brighter the light grew, fueled by
the rhythm
The cold lifeless hand twitched
The light and dark hovered over the body
The body being on the line between light and
dark

*****

For the next couple of months, my life turned around dramatically. My mom reconnected with Cierra and me and apologized for
disappearing. She was, in fact, with a new guy; but she wanted us
to start coming over every other weekend with the girls, Jalena and
Julissa, as well as Alex. In addition, I no longer had a life outside of
my house. I slept and ate all my meals alone after making them or
serving myself a plate. I also continuously asked permission to do
basic things, such as, shower, do homework, go to school, and to go
to bed. I was a walking puppet with no innards.

I heard arguments constantly between Dad and Tonya about
how she found different boarding schools for me for special needs.
Each time I heard them talking about them (specifically one in

Washington), I would ask my vision teacher about it. She was trying to send me away; but unfortunately for her, these schools would not take me because I was not intellectually impaired—it was just my vision that was impaired.

Part of me hoped that I could go just to get away from the house; but on the other hand, I would miss things. The only solace I had anymore were with my friends at school. But even then, I was becoming a shell of a person again trapped in a cage. Constant threats, verbal abuse, name-calling, and mental abuse plagued me.

One weekend, while visiting my mom, she sat me on her bed and asked me if I was happy. Looking up at her, I faked a smile and said yes. She immediately knew that I was lying. "Well, I can see you are not happy. Let me know if you want to talk," she told me. Fear won out, so I didn't say anything. I wanted to desperately say, "Don't let me go back!" But at the same time, I felt like if I said anything, it would reach the ears of Dad and Tonya.

Since Dad was constantly on the road doing biker stuff, he was barely home. If anything, he would be home for maybe a week; then he'd go back out, where no one would see him. Cierra and I were constantly with Tonya, and my fear primarily took place because I knew that Tonya despised me and there was no one to back me up. I kept thinking, *If I said anything, what would be the repercussions?*

After the weekend was over, I returned home, where the tension was high. I hated this house and everything that it stood for. All I saw when I looked was hatefulness, yellow smoke-encrusted walls from the constant chain-smoking, and devious plans to incriminate and abuse me. I was constantly called hurtful names. I was constantly manipulated into saying things that weren't even true because they believed it to be true. I was tired of it and no longer wanted to be at home.

Sitting in the back by myself once again, Tonya called me out and told me that I could sit in the living room with the rest of the family again. It shocked me. I had no idea where it came from. The only thing I could think of was that my mother called my father and complained about how I looked sad. That worried me, though. Anytime I looked sad in front of another family member, I was yelled at for that too. I didn't want to sit in the living room, though. I just wanted to be left to pace in my cage, away from prying and hateful eyes.

Pacing back and forth in the kids' room, I sang "Jesus Loves Me." Tears began to fill my eyes, and I just wanted to collapse on the floor and die. I could no longer live like this. I needed something to live for. I no longer had anything. Since I was showing signs of depression, I had a long and stern talking to about how I need to stop moping around. The only words that I could hear were "you're stupid," "you're retarded," "you're gaining weight," and "you are being sent to a different school."

I grew weary and tired. I paced one more time, singing "Jesus Loves Me." Then I stopped halfway. I no longer thought so. I no longer thought Jesus was there because I was in pain. I was crushed and beaten, and my hope dwindled out of existence. As I thought this and stopped singing, I heard a voice to my right say, "He loves you so." I stood shocked. I looked in that direction and realized that no one was there. I could not see anyone there, but I was sure I heard a voice. I felt a spark of something. Before, I had nothing left; and now, suddenly, there was something there. Renewed with hope, I continued singing and praying.

*****

The school year was almost over. We had only a month left, but it felt like a lifetime. I was still grounded and caged in my house like an animal. It was sunny and bright, and I wanted to be out and about with my friends. The only outside time I would get, though, is when I sat out front in a chair with Tonya. Cierra and I continually saw our mother every other weekend. While sitting on her bed one weekend, the three of us chatted. Cierra and I were depressed and feeling caged. Our father was always on trips with other individuals riding motorcycles, and he was gone for weeks at a time.

"Are you guys happy?" our mother asked.

Cierra and I both shook our heads no and said that we were not. We told her what was happening in the house—how I was constantly called names, how Cierra felt like Tonya hated her, and how everyone was constantly fighting.

"Do you want to come live with me?"

Cierra responded yes right away. It was easy for her. It was a little harder for me because not only was I suffering in the hands of Dad and Tonya; but I was also told horrible things about my mom and how she would never let me see my friends, go out of the house, or do anything.

"Can we move to Quakertown?"

"We can try."

After saying yes, my mom said that she would get us out of that house.

One day, after school, my mom called Rob's cell phone before I got on the bus. She said, "I got a PFA to get you guys out of the house. Go home, pack all your clothes and things, and get ready. I am coming to get you." Excitement and dread coiled in my stomach like a snake ready to strike. I was excited to leave this dreadful house, but I was also very much afraid. If I ever did something that was against Tonya and Dad's rules, it would be the end of me.

I slowly walked down the steps of the bus and walked into my house after saying hi to Tonya. She sat outside in her chair reading a book and smoking. Quickly, I ran upstairs and grabbed all my things that I could and shoved them into a wash basket and in backpacks. Cierra came up the stairs to do the same. After some time, we sat together on my bed, watching out the window and waiting for our mom. We both grew anxious and fearful of what would happen if one of our other siblings saw us with our bags packed. Thankfully, Hali was at a friend's house, and Brianna and JJ were not home.

Before long, pulling up out front was our mom's SUV. After grabbing our baskets and bags, Cierra and I rushed downstairs, hoping to escape without notice. Opening the door, I was disappointed to see Tonya on the phone. Cierra confidently walked by Tonya with her stuff without saying a word. However, as I tried to rush by, I was not afforded the same luxury.

Thrusting the phone in my hand, Tonya demanded I speak to my father on the phone. All I could comprehend was him yelling things like "GET IN THE FUCKING HOUSE!" or "DO NOT LEAVE THAT HOUSE!" and "YOUR MOTHER WILL NEVER LET YOU HANG OUT WITH YOUR FRIENDS!" Over and over, these words were pounded into my head through the phone. The yelling from both Dad and Tonya petrified me.

Walking back into the house, I sat on the steps hysterically crying and praying to God. I wanted him to do what needed to be done. If I was truly meant to leave this house, I wanted him to make it happen. I was too terrified to do it myself. Rob came in after me, taking my hand and telling me to go. "She's waiting for you," he said. I knew she was, but I did not know anymore what I was supposed to do. While admitting this to him, a police officer came into the house and kneeled in front of me.

"Your mom has a PFA for your stepmom and father. You have to go with her," he said. I felt like my prayer was answered. Even if I was forced back into my dad's house, he couldn't punish me since it was the police officer telling me this information. Standing up, I walked out of the house with Rob, past Tonya, and into my mom's car. I got in and sat next to Cierra, and we looked out the window as we pulled away from the place we hated and were terrified of so much.

17.5 Years Old

The hopes of the godly result in happiness, but
the expectations of the wicked come to nothing.
—Proverbs 10:28 NLT

Life is serious enough we need to be reminded
to laugh together to help ease the tension
that builds up in our lives. Laughter is a
great reminder of the joy that is hidden in
our day to day lives. In the Bible, Nehemiah,
encourages the people by telling them the joy
in the Lord is our strength. Strength is not
being so busy or being so put together you
don't have time to crack a smile. Strength
comes when we slow down enough to
experience God's joy in our lives. If you are
at your brink, pause and take time laugh.
—The Daily Bible Devotion App

Eight months later

I shifted from one lifestyle to the next. This lifestyle was drastically different. Since my mother worked the night shift, my sister and I were home alone during the nights. Of course, we had rules; and we had our family friend, Rich, who was like a second father to us as an emergency contact—but it wasn't the same. Slowly, I transformed from this scared, beaten-up caterpillar to a beautiful butterfly. I wore clothes appropriate for my age, not the clothes that were baggy and childish like the ones that were picked out for me.

I met and made new friends, who helped me transition from one school to the other. I still had my best friends, Julia, Amber, and Belinda; but now I could add to that list. I no longer felt awkward and weird sitting with my laptop and other equipment in the new school. I felt like I was simply accepted and not judged. However, as things began to turn around for the good for me in this new situation, it began to create drama in my relationship with Robert.

One day, I had to open the door way too early in the morning. My mouth gaped upon seeing Robert standing in the hallway of my apartment building.

"ROBERT, WHAT ARE YOU DOING HERE?"

"I walked since you don't come over anymore."

I was so shocked that he decided to walk ten miles from where he lived on a highway to where I lived currently. I let him into the apartment. We spoke and hung out; then, after a while, I tried to break it off with him again. I was beginning to feel trapped. No matter what I did, said, or how I reacted to him trying to kiss me, he still clung on like I was his lifeline.

Each weekend, he asked me to come over. I always either said no or went because I felt guilty. I wanted it to just end, and I just felt terrible for dragging it out. I wanted to wipe this page clean and continue moving on in my new life. I began to discover that I did love Robert in a way, but I do not think I was actually *in* love with him.

*****

As the year progressed, I began to develop a crush on a boy in my class. He was tall, slender, with dirty-blonde hair; and I was enthralled. Several different times, I tried to get his attention. With the junior prom quickly approaching, I thought that my best chance was to invite him as my date. Sitting and reading my Facebook messages of the two of us talking, I was disappointed that he had said he did not want to go to prom. Disappointed, I wracked my brain for another way to get him to hang out or talk to me. I eventually typed back, "No worries I understand. But maybe we could be friends instead?" He replied, "Yes." I felt a little victory and fist-bumped the air.

I looked down at my little green flip phone as I saw it vibrating with Robert's picture on the screen. Sighing, I answered, "Hello." He asked, "Hi. Are we still dating?" I scribbled on a piece of paper as I held the phone to my ear, thinking of a plan to get it through to him that we had to be over. An idea struck me like a light bulb flickering on above my head. It was unethical, but it would help me break it off with him once and for all. I invited Rob to come to my prom, knowing that one of my friends, Courtney, would be able to hook me up with another boy to take as a date.

*****

Weaving through tables, I held my date's hand as he led me toward the stairs, where the dance floor was. Out of nowhere, Robert grabbed my hand. "I want to talk."

"Now? It's prom. I want to dance and have fun."

"Yes, now. We need to talk about us."

"Robert, I don't want to talk about us."

As I said these words, I watched his facial expression change from one of sorrow to one of anger. After calling me a bitch, he left the building. I felt bad for what I did. However, after trying to break up with him multiple times and him just not accepting it, I did not know what else to do.

*****

A burning heat consumed me as I thought about my new crush, Eric. I was jumping from the end of one relationship and trying to jump to another. We frequently hung out, but I wanted more. Praying to the Lord each day and night, I began asking him to allow me to date Eric, to be his girlfriend—but first and foremost, for Eric to like me back. I didn't care to ask God what his thoughts were or what his will was. I just knew what this consuming feeling told me, and I wanted to appease it.

I opened the door to my bedroom and slowly walked in. I felt the tension and the horror mounting inside of me as my eyes swept from one side of the room to the other. A dresser stood parallel to me, hiding the bed from view. Blood painted the walls of the bedroom and salt decorated the floor. A wheezing voice sounded from where the bed sat. In the middle of the bed lay an injured man. "You're pouring salt into my wounds," he said.

I sat straight up in bed and looked around. Perpendicular to me, I saw my sister sleeping in her bed. Everything was fine and normal. However, the dream I just had was not normal. Lying back, I thought of what the dream meant. As I prayed to try and go back to sleep, I heard the Lord clear as day in my head say that he did not want me to date Eric.

18 Years Old

The hopes of the godly result in happiness, but
the expectations of the wicked come to nothing.
—Proverbs 10:28 NLT

Life is serious enough we need to be reminded
to laugh together to help ease the tension
that builds up in our lives. Laughter is a
great reminder of the joy that is hidden in
our day to day lives. In the Bible, Nehemiah,
encourages the people by telling them the
joy in the Lord is our strength. Strength is
not being so busy or being so put together
you don't have any time to crack a smile.
Strength comes when we slow down enough
to experience God's joy in our lives. If you are
at your brink, pause and take time laugh.
—The Daily Bible Devotion App

Several months later

Months had gone by, and I got exactly what I prayed for. I was now
dating Eric and was happy. My confidence began to build, and I was
becoming bolder toward my mom. My mom was still working the
night shift but was trying to switch to the day shift. She gained custody of my younger siblings, Julissa and Jalena, which made it harder
on me. Until she switched to the day shift, I had to bathe, help Julissa
with her homework, heat up or make dinner, and then also do my
own homework. It was challenging, and I started to rebel against it.

To make matters worse, my mom and her boyfriend, Elvis, began fighting. Most of the time, it was behind closed doors, but it eventually started to trickle out and into the open. Their yelling tickled my ears as Cierra and I woke up. Our mom was throwing Elvis out again. Yet each time she threw him out, he ended up worming his way back in. This time, as he grappled with my mom, he claimed that he would do better. "Better" turned into drinking each weekend and inevitably turned into Elvis's brother chasing me and Cierra up into our room. I began to hate these games. However, each time I tried to talk to my mom about the issue, she replied, "He wouldn't do that."

*****

As Eric and I grew closer, I also grew further apart from not only God but also my mother. She finally switched to day shift, which helped tremendously. I was no longer plagued with taking care of things at night. However, we were still required to babysit after school for about an hour and a half, when she got done work. It wasn't a big deal; but to a teenager who was enthralled with a boy and wanted to spend time with him, it became tedious.

My mom developed a drinking problem, and it began to affect me and Cierra. Each weekend, Elvis and his brother would drink with my mom and her friend. Hispanic music blasted from the TV; and although we didn't mind the music, we minded the company. From time to time, Elvis's brother would chase us up to our room, where we locked ourselves in. I became eager for my birthday to come so that I could get away from it all.

As time went on, my mom began to be abused by Elvis. Instead of kicking him out, she married him. Shock and disbelief filled me up, and I couldn't believe what Cierra found out and told me. We despised the man, and we wanted our mother to leave him. I understood that she had a hard time raising four out of the five kids she currently had custody of as a single mother, but marrying the guy… Once we confronted her, we also learned that she was yet again pregnant with another baby.

This further strengthened my resolve to want to move out at eighteen. As my birthday approached, things with Eric escalated. I was only consumed with selfish thoughts of what I wanted to do and not looking at the bigger picture. I disregarded my God and didn't even ask him for his thoughts on the matter. Instead, I did what I wanted, and I moved in with Eric in an effort to take control of my life.

*****

Over the next few months, my life was filled with passion, lust, fire, and excitement. The fire burned hot and fierce between me and Eric. We grew together in ways I didn't know was possible. I not only grew with Eric; but I also formed a special bond with his mom, Sandy. She became a close friend; and I often helped her with things around the house, Eric's sister Liz (who was disabled), and many other things. I felt in control, complete, and unbeatable. I gave my whole heart to Eric, and it beat for him.

Although my happiness was at its prime, my headaches and eyesight were a different case. When I was back at CHOP for another visit with Dr. Phillips and Dr. Liu, they had determined that my eyesight had deteriorated once more; however, fortunately, there was no tumor growth. After discussing the matter with their other colleagues, Dr. Phillips and Dr. Liu felt that chamber was necessary.

Driving back to Philadelphia the next week, we took a tour of the hyperbaric chamber. Walking through what looked like an old high school hallway, with blue lockers, we found a brown oak door. We entered a small waiting room with brown padded chairs. A young woman with chin-length black hair smiled at us.

"You must be Samantha and her parents."

"Grandparents, yes," my grandmother replied.

"Let me show you around."

Following the peppy young woman, we walked into the other room, where there were TV screens monitoring the inside of the chamber. There were all types of buttons and cords that linked to the chamber.

"This is the tech area to monitor and chamber. Once in the chamber, the air levels drop as if you were going 250 feet below sea level. Once under, air masks go on to the patients, and they are in there for two hours."

It was thought that the hyperbaric chamber could heal my optic nerves from the possible radiation damage and recover the little eyesight that had been lost. Dr. Phillips and Dr. Liu believed that the slight loss of my vision occurred through the radiation treatment done to the tumor right around my optic nerves.

New appointments were set up, and I was to begin treatment the next week. I needed to do it six days a week for a month to see if this helped. The hyperbaric chamber did not seem too bad; however, I began to fear the possibility of becoming completely blind.

I climbed the steps up to Eric and my bedroom and opened the door to find Eric sitting at his computer. Normally we would exchange words; but as I tried to speak to him, only silence greeted me. Sitting on the floor, I peered up at him, waiting for him to say something. Instead, the song, "Let It Die" by Three Days Grace played and "spoke" to me. I understood what he was trying to say. Tears filled my eyes and began to spill over. I begged and pleaded with him to speak to me; however, only silence filled the small room.

"We had fire in our eyes…" went the song. It was so true. In the beginning, we had so much fire between us that it was so hard to stay away from each other. However, a new lyric caught my attention. "I just don't wanna hear it anymore…I just don't care about you anymore." Sobs racked my body, and I couldn't control it. I felt like my world was crashing, and there was no way of stopping it. I lived with him, and now I had to figure something else out. What my mom said was going to happen, happened. Praying to the Lord that night, I heard him say to go live with my Nanny.

*****

Months later

As I threw my graduation cap up into the air with the rest of my class, I was ecstatic to be done with high school. I was officially going to Kutztown University and was ready to move on with my life. Celebrating with my friends and family, I closed a chapter in my life. I reconnected with my mom and was able to look past what had happened between us. She was trying to be better too—not drinking or having parties anymore. I had a new baby brother named Anthony, and my eyesight was stable once more from the hyperbaric chamber. I was happy and ready to move on and attend Kutztown University.

One weekend, I went home for a birthday party. It was one of my siblings' birthday party, so my mom invited a whole bunch of kids over. As I sat on my mom's kitchen floor with Alex, his two friends Ashley and Devin sat with us laughing and talking. After the party, I walked with my brother and his two friends back to Devin's house. Suddenly, Devin turned to me and asked me out. Smiling, I shook my head no. He was sixteen, and I was eighteen. Although this would not have been a big deal in several years, I just wasn't ready after my relationship with Eric.

As I returned home each weekend, I would see Devin. He became a fixture in my life, just like my brother Alex. Seeing the childish side to Devin reinforced my decision to keep saying no to him. However, when Devin and I were alone, I could see a more mature side. He was charming and allowed me to feel beautiful again. Keeping him as a friend boosted my self-esteem, and I was grateful for it.

While hanging out with Alex one day, he begged me to go out with Devin. "Sam, please. He really likes you."

"I'm not ready, Alex. I just ended with my relationship with Eric."

"It's been months. You should date now."

Seeing my brother literally beg me to date Devin broke me, so I said yes. Thus, I texted Devin that I would date him with his parents' permission. They gave it willingly since they too grew close to me.

I babysat their other two children frequently and became a family friend.

*****

Halloween came. Although I had agreed to date Devin, my heart was not in it. He was merely just a distraction from the relationship I had ended with Eric. I used it to my advantage to hang out with my brother Alex, as well as Ashley, their other friend. I began to feel normal again, and I enjoyed the distraction and steam I was able to let off when I returned home on the weekends from school.

During the Halloween parade, I made plans to go back to Devin's house to hang out with his family. As we sat on the couch listening to music, Devin's father came out from the kitchen with drinks in his hand. I took the drink from Devin's dad and began drinking it. It was really good. The chocolate flavor burst in my tongue. As I kept on drinking, I began to feel fuzzy, clumsy, and giggly. As my judgment became more impaired, I realized I was drinking a type of alcoholic chocolate milk. I liked it, but I had never had it before.

I headed to Devin's room with him, and we thought it would be best for me to sleep over instead of walk home late at night while intoxicated. Moments after slipping into bed with Devin, I began to feel his hands roam my body. I rolled toward him and moved my hands too. Spinning, flipping, a spiritual battle overtook me. Wanting to fill the void that was in my heart, I roamed my hands toward places that I should not have. Thoughts overtook my brain. *No... Not good... Should not...* But the void inside me and the alcohol won over.

19 Years Old

They were calling out to each other, Holy
Holy Holy is the Lord of Heaven's armies.
The whole Earth is filled with his glory.
—Isaiah 6:3 NLT

Today we should be thankful for all the
blessings we are given. The Lord our God gives
us blessings in many different ways. Many of
these blessings may be given in mysterious ways
that may not look like a blessing at first. Give
thanks to our God for the blessings he showers
us with. Praise his name and give thanks.
—The Daily Bible Devotion App

Sitting in the bathroom, my friends and I chatted about our periods and how they were in sync with one another. I laughed as I walked over to the stall. My mind began racing, trying to figure out when the last time was that I got my period. As I sat on the toilet, I looked down at the water in the bowl. Then I looked at the toilet paper. There was nothing. But all my friends got theirs, and I always got mine right around the same time as Chelsea's. I shook off the worry, figuring that it must be late due to the stress of finals.

Lying in bed one night, I rolled around, trying to figure out why I couldn't sleep. Pain shot through my pelvis like intense cramps. Relieved that I was having cramps, thinking that my period was coming, I prayed for sleep to overcome me.

The next couple of nights, I continued to feel those horrible cramps. Each time I woke up, I looked to see if I had my period;

but there was no evidence of pointing to that conclusion. I decided to take a walk around campus that night. Looking up at the stars, I asked my old friend God why I was experiencing these cramps and why I had not gotten my period yet. Gazing up into the beautiful dark sky, I heard a voice in my head.

The voice was clear, but my emotions clouded what I had heard. Looking up into the sky, where all the stars gazed down at me, twinkling in the black sky, I begged God to not let it be true. I couldn't bear to hear what God was telling me. Pacing back and forth outside my dorm building, I pleaded and begged with God to not let it be true. His answer remained the same. Denial poisoned my brain; and refusing to acknowledge what he was telling me, I pushed the thoughts away and hid it deep within myself.

*****

Walking around campus, I began to feel out of breath. I became winded, and it was unusual for me to feel that way. Walking around the campus was never such a feat for me. As my windedness increased, so did pains in my breasts. I knew what was happening; but instead of acknowledging it, I denied it. I didn't want it. I only had just turned nineteen. I had a whole life ahead of me. Pushing it back in my mind, I continued to deny, ignore, and pretend to be happy.

The winter break came, and I was home for a month. As I was walking into my doctor's office for a physical, I thought that maybe I was developing diabetes because my father had diabetes. "When was your last period," she asked. I told her, "In October." So she asked me to do a pregnancy test. While waiting back in the room, I prayed and prayed to the Lord for the test to come back negative. What felt like an hour (which was really only about five minutes), my doctor returned with a grim face. "Sam, your test came back positive."

I wish I could say I was shocked; however, I was only terrified. God told me I was pregnant, and I refused to believe it. I stared at her, waiting for her to say something else. Nothing came but another bucket of ice-cold water over my head. "Abortion…" My answer was *no* right away. I didn't want to do abortion. I had no idea what I was going to do, but abortion was off the table.

Noises were muffled, my brain stopped, and I had no idea what to do next. She gathered information about pregnancy for me and allowed me to look into some different options. After gathering the information, I began to do my research. I wanted to cry, scream, and hide from the world. I felt like I let my grandparents down, I let God down, and I let myself down.

*****

One afternoon, I walked from my Nanny's home, where I lived, to Walmart. Altogether, it was about a fifteen-minute walk. As I walked up the hill, I saw a familiar tall figure walking down the hill toward me. My heart stuttered, and I became aware of him switching sides to avoid me. As Eric and I passed by each other, nothing was said, but I felt something. Knowing that I had feelings still, I needed fifteen minutes to admit to myself that Devin was nothing more than a rebound. Unfortunately, I would hurt his feelings; but between the news I had for him and how my heart was still sore and aching, I didn't want to go further. I didn't even want to do the things we did that one night.

I felt despair, sadness, and depression envelop me. As I got to Walmart to get my prenatal vitamins, my phone shrieked with an incoming text. Eric's name flashed on the screen, and he was asking if I wanted to get together with him. Without thinking, my thumbs flew over the keyboard, and I replied with a yes right away. A tiny bit of hope soared in my chest as I made plans to get together with Eric on Christmas Eve.

Fighting erupts all around me when I tell Devin and his parents about my pregnancy. It was confirmed with an ultrasound. Joy came from seeing the tiny heartbeat flutter on the monitors, but anxiety and nervousness came from having to reveal not only to Devin and his family the news but also to my grandparents. My grandparents were a big part of my life, and I never wanted to upset them. This felt like a huge step backward, and I would definitely disappoint them with the news of my pregnancy out of wedlock.

"We want a paternity test," states Karen, Devin's mom. My heart was being ripped all over again. The family I grew so close to, developed a comfort in, was threatening me. If I didn't leave them alone and didn't stop saying that the baby was Devin's, then Karen threatened to charge me with rape charges on her son so I could never have a career. I felt awful. I didn't know what I deserved to be treated in such a way. I was called so many names, like slut and whore, that it was like I was back at my father's house with him and my stepmom. Instead, I walked away and let them feel what they wanted to feel. I decided that I was going to raise the baby on my own.

*****

Walking over to Eric's house, I tugged on my sweatshirt to hide the tiny belly I was beginning to develop. I was already starting to show, and I was only two and a half months along. I wasn't even that far; but my stomach started to develop a bump, and I became self-conscious about it. Sitting on the couch with Eric, we chatted about all the things that we missed in each other's lives. We caught up, went for a walk in the freezing cold, and laughed. It was almost like old times.

One night became two nights a week, then more and more as time went on. We began texting again, hanging out, and spending a lot of time together. My feelings began to grow again. I couldn't help it even though I knew it was wrong, and we had already broken up once. One night, he told me he felt the same. Guilt hit me like a train because of the secret I was hiding. I wanted to run and hide instead of telling someone else, but I knew he needed to know if we had another chance of being together. I just wanted to tell my grandparents first.

Gathering one afternoon in my grandparents' living room, my sisters Brianna and Cierra sat opposite my grandfather. My dad and Tonya were in the area and in the same house. I told them weeks ago that I was pregnant when they texted one day to see how I was. As

I sat there, waiting to say something, I clenched my hands together waiting. My legs bounced, my hands began picking at the skin around my nails, and I began to think that maybe I could hide it from them somehow.

Walking into the room with my father, my grandmother sat down next to me and patted my leg. My father looked at my grandfather and said, "Sam's pregnant." My grandfather's mouth dropped open, and I could feel the shock and sadness wafting off him. They began talking in circles about what I was going to do and how it was a mistake. Overwhelmed, I got up and ran down the steps to the front door and down their backyard behind their huge barn.

I was overwhelmed with sadness. I didn't know how to handle my emotions, what my grandparents thought of me now, and what my next steps would be. I felt the grief begin to build; and my mind filled with anxiety, depression, and the sense of the fight-or-flight reaction. I wanted to flee in this instance, though. I wanted to flee to where no one could find me. I was this huge disappointment to my family. I was the only one thus far who had actually graduated high school and attended college in our family, and I felt like an embarrassment and disappointment. I tried to call some friends to talk to them, but no one answered or were too busy. Feeling like I had no one, I looked back up to the sky calling out for God. He was so far away, but I could hear him. I was going to be okay.

*****

Sitting with Eric on his bed, I took in a long breath before I told him.

"Hey, Eric, I need to tell you something."

Looking at me, he said, "Go ahead."

"Please don't judge or anything. Just hear me out."

As I told him how I was pregnant, he asked how it happened.

"One night, I was intoxicated, and I was hanging out with my friend Devin...and I was raped."

Hugging me, he let me cry on his shoulder. Although I didn't actually say the word *no* out loud to Devin, in a way, I felt like he took a piece of me. He pressed into me when I was vulnerable, so I in my mind declared it as rape. I felt better telling him, but I was too nervous to let any of his family members know because of the judgment.

Months went by. I was going through many trials of learning what it was like to be pregnant. I was determined to keep the baby and somehow raise it on my own while going to college, not working, and living at my Nanny's on her couch. Things were not adding up in my head, but I had no idea what else to do. All I knew was that this was my responsibility, so I had to figure it out.

Then one day, I sat with my aunt Jen for dinner, and she told me of a different option: adoption. My aunt Jen was adopted by my grandparents because at first my grandmother could not have children. Thus, she adopted my father and my aunt Jen. After, as a miracle, she ended up pregnant with my aunt Jessica. Jen told me about adoption and how there are so many families without children because they couldn't have them. That she felt blessed to be adopted, and it may be something that I consider as well.

My relationship with Eric continued. We were officially back together, but as I started to show more and more, his family began to notice and began to make judgments. Eric and his sister Tanya fought over sticky notes posted to his bedroom door about me. She wanted nothing to do with me and wanted our relationship to end. However, Eric was understanding and knew I was looking into other options. Fuses became short; and multiple times, there were verbal fights about how I may be trapping him and how he didn't deserve someone like me.

I began to feel horrible, like I was being sucked into a hole. I was trying so hard to hold it together. However, each time I was attacked because of my pregnancy, a piece of me began to break apart. I hated myself for who and what I was. All I saw when I looked in a mirror was shattered glass and fragments of who I used to be.

*****

Sitting on an empty school bus, I sat in the large bench seat holding a little baby boy in my arms. Smiling at it, I felt pure joy. Looking toward my left side, I saw a woman sitting there with me, gazing at the baby with pure love and joy. Turning to look back at the baby, I asked, "Do you want to go back to Tami?" The baby shook his head yes, and I handed him back over to her.

Waking up, I opened the different profiles on my computer that I received the night before from the adoption agency I was in contact with. The first name that popped up in the many different profiles were Tami and Herald. Shocked, I clicked through the other names to make sure before coming back to Tami. They were a lovely older couple. Both professors at a college and well established. They both were religious, and that made me feel better. I fell in love with them instantly. I knew in my heart this was the couple that God wanted my beautiful baby to go to. Looking up at the stars, I felt God tell me that he was a boy and that he was a child of God.

Sitting in Eric's room with him, I was happy to report that I had finished the semester. I was happy to be done. I was seven months pregnant, and I was exhausted. It was getting harder and harder to move around. The fights continued between Eric and his sister, but his mom accepted what was happening since I was committed to giving my little baby boy to Herald and Tami. I chose an open adoption with them and couldn't be happier of whom God had chosen for me. I felt God even though I was with Eric again. I felt him. I was not as close to him as I used to be, but I knew he was still with me.

*****

Looking down at a beautiful baby boy, I felt pride, joy, sorrow, and happiness. It was saddening knowing that I was going to walk out of the hospital without the beautiful baby in my arms, but looking at Herald and Tami and the tears in their eyes full of joy that they were finally receiving a baby…it gave me the encouragement that I needed. I knew it was God's will to have little baby Michael to be Tami and Herald's child. I knew Michael would know who I was since it was an open adoption; and I knew one day, I would have other children with my future husband.

Going home was the hardest thing I ever had to do. Walking Michael back to the nursery in the hospital, I handed him over and left. Crying the whole way home, I knew it was the right thing to do. I just knew God was with me, but walking away from my beautiful baby no matter how he was conceived hurt my heart in so many ways. I felt sorrow and pain but also relief.

That night, Eric had plans to go out with a friend to see a midnight movie. Staying in his room, I locked the door because his aunt and sister were over. They both were not a fan of me, and I just wanted to be left alone. My heart was still aching, and I just wanted to recuperate from the birthing process. Banging sounded on the door as I was watching TV. When I opened the door, I came face to face with his Aunt Sherry.

"You need to leave," she said.

Looking at her, I couldn't comprehend what was going on.

"You don't belong here. You aren't going to open your legs and trap Eric with another baby like you did that poor boy that you slept with came this baby."

Shocked, I replied, "I did the right thing in doing adoption, and I didn't trap anyone. Eric and I aren't even having sex. I literally just had a baby!"

Shouting at me, she called me a whore and that I needed to leave in the next ten minutes or she was calling the cops. Crying, I tried to call Eric. However, he didn't answer, so I left a message. Packing my stuff, I headed downstairs and looked at Sandy, his mother.

Since I lived with Sandy in the past, I grew very close to her. Looking at Sandy, I asked her why. Anytime I have slept over or taken any food or drinks, I always replaced it with a whole new gallon or bag, or whatever it may have been. I wasn't comprehending what was going on. I was already so broken that my mind was just not working. Being called bitch, whore, squatter…these were all things that I heard in the past and never deserved. Running out the door crying, I ran to Alex's house, where Rich and Lisa were.

Lisa was Rich's new girlfriend, and I became very close to her over the time I was not speaking with my mom. She became my second mom, and I cared for her and her son Nik just as much as I cared for Alex and Rich. Walking over toward their house, I called my brother Alex; and he let me in their house. Bawling my eyes out, I explained to them what had happened.

I wasn't homeless. I still lived with my Nanny, but I didn't want to be there or alone. I thought maybe being at Rich and Lisa's house would give me greater comfort. Falling asleep that night, I began to plot how I was going to get my own apartment and then have Eric move in with me. I was tired of being called names that had no meaning to the type of person I was. I wanted to be my own person and respected as an adult like everyone else.

20 Years Old

"Does not my word burn like fire?" says
the Lord. "Is it not like a mighty hammer
that smashes a rock to pieces?"
—Jeremiah 23:29 NLT

The Bible is a wonderful tool that we have
been blessed with. It is God's word and
direction to us. It can calm fears and convict
heavy hearts. Are you staying tuned in to
what God is saying to you? Be faithful to the
Lord and see what he can do in your life.
—The Daily Bible Devotion App

Living in my own apartment was tougher than what I thought it would be. Having God's Word to afford food, bills, utilities, and other necessities was a challenge. Luckily, I had some help from my grandparents and Rich and Lisa. Rich gave me all his old kitchen utensils and table since he was now living with Lisa. My grandparents purchased a fridge and helped me get a washer and dryer. In addition, they helped with transporting my new bed that I had to buy and getting things set up. It was a whole new experience.

For months, Eric and I lived off of canned foods, some freezer things, and basically anything cheap. It was rare when I actually made meats because things were so expensive. It was hard paying rent, electric, phone, cable, and then food on my own. I was only receiving Supplementary Security Income (SSI). Eric on the other hand only forked out maybe $150 a month. I was barely making it each month and on top of that I was back at Kutztown continuing my education.

Our fire was snuffed out and gone. Eric hid in the darkness away from me. Seeing that the fire was out, I tried to use alternatives to relight the flame. Giving him any spare money that I had, I thought it could buy his love. Nights grew cold and quiet. We barely talked and each time I tried to talk to him about our problems or what was bothering him he never answered. After months of living together from August to March, I thought it would be different. However, our relationship turned even more different than what I thought.

Dinner plans were canceled, spending time together became sitting in the same room just watching television, and the connection became mute. I became desperate. I began researching what would be wrong with our relationship. When I got nothing out of the Internet, I began to cry each night on our couch as he played video games in the next room.

Huddled in a ball, I cried out to him asking him why and to save me. I wanted to be held and coddled. I wanted the Lord to provide for me and help me get back to him. I just didn't know how. I became a lost sheep once more and I couldn't find my way back.

*****

Applying to one of the local Walmart, I began working as the apparel girl. I wanted to sustain myself and I was tired of not receiving any money form Eric. I was basically paying for everything in the apartment by myself and barely making it. The first month went off with a bang. I made some new friends and I learned many different new techniques. I loved the little family that I developed in the apparel department, and I loved going to work. One day while manning the fitting room, a redheaded boy walked up to the desk and got some tape to fix a shoebox. Looking at him, I smiled. Smiling back, we said nothing and kept working.

Each time I saw him, I checked him out. He was tall, thin, had beautiful blue eyes and long orange hair. I was attracted to him, but we hadn't even talked yet! Looking at my new friend Sierra one day, I asked her who he was.

"Oh, that's Brent."

"Oh, he's cute!"

"Yeah, he is good-looking, but he's an uber Christian…"

Not knowing what that meant to her, it piqued my interest.

Over the next month, Brent and I worked in silence with one another, but stole glances, smiles, and would work close together on team zones. Watching him put away shoes in the correct spots near where I was working, I spun Around the corner and inhaled a lungful of courage.

"So I heard you wanted to see the new *Ironman* movie?"

"Yeah, I do."

Taking a chance, I smiled, looked up at him, and replied, "I'll go with you if you want." I held my breath and waited for his response.

"Oh, I am actually going with another friend."

I felt dejected at his response. "Oh…well, let me know if he cancels."

"I will."

My hope was crushed. I felt a little sad, but I was okay.

The next day as I walked into the fitting room, Brent was standing twirling the keys to the fitting room around his finger.

"Were you manning the fitting room until I got here?"

"Yeah, I was the first on schedule…Oh, uh, were you still interested in going to see *Ironman* with me?"

Giddiness filled my stomach and I had to calm my inner monolog of fist pumping and screaming yes.

"Sure. What happened to your friend?"

"He wanted to go out with another girl."

Setting up plans, we made a plan to go on a date that weekend.

As Brent and I got to know one another from the next several dates and working together, we encountered challenges at work. Our boss found out we were dating and was looking for a reason to fire me. He blamed me for Brent not getting four pallets in four hours done by himself. In reality, that was hard for one of the other managers to do by themselves. Switching to a different department, my job was secured.

Our relationship began to grow from a flickering light of interest to a large ball of light. We made boundaries, rules, and held one another to God's standards of no adultery, I felt like I was worth something for this man to actually respect me for who I am. We spoke about my past and who I was today. I told him how I believed in God, but I needed help finding him again. Accepting my past and my faults, he helped me find the Lord again.

*****

Each Sunday we attended church together. My heart and spirit were becoming whole and I began to feel alive again. Walking into church the first time was like having an electric paddle to my chest and being electrocuted back to life. I began to feel God. I began to read his Word, and I began to hear his words. I was becoming thirsty, and only he could quench my thirst.

Brent and my relationship grew not only in a spiritual sense, but also in a way that allowed us to call one another best friend. It was nothing like Eric and my relationship when we first started to date. My relationship with Eric was like an explosion of fire that just burnt out in the end. Brent and my relationship however...It was like a slow building fire. One that grew with each passing day. I was respected, loved, and treated as an equal. Not only was I treated well, but I was not required to perform. In fact, we did things the right way by following God's commandments and what he wanted for us.

One morning I woke up and went out to my living room where Eric was sitting at our kitchen table. Turning to the fridge to get a drink of milk, he asked who Brent was. I had already told Brent who Eric really was. However, I had not told Eric. Each time I tried to talk to him, he wouldn't respond. He would turn me away, and I was left bleeding all over our couch.

"No one," I replied.

"DON'T LIE TO ME!" he shouted.

Jumping, I turned to see he was on my laptop going through my Facebook messenger and reading our private conversations.

"He's my boyfriend."

"So you're cheating on me. You lied and cheated on me!"

"Eric, you don't talk to me. We haven't talked in months. Each time I tried to talk to you, you blew me off. Each time we made plans to do something, you would go out with your friends or play video games."

We both went quiet. Sitting there, he looked at me. "You're right. I am sorry. I think it was my way of ending our relationship without having to actually end it."

That night after I returned home from work, his stuff was gone out of our apartment and nothing was left of him.

*****

After dating for six months, it became clear that God wanted us to take a break. Obeying his will, we broke up. I didn't know why, but God wanted me to wait and take a step back from my relationship with Brent. The first time we broke up, we were back together after three days. We wanted to be together. We loved one another and knew that something was different about this relationship. Hearing God again, we broke up for a second time and stayed apart for two months.

Although we were a part as a couple, we were still very much best friends. We still spent time with one another, but rather spending our time kissing, hugging, or making googly eyes at each other, we read the Bible went to church, and spent time with God. Finally, after that two-month period, we got back together. Rewarded, we found that our relationship was so much sweeter because we both had God at our center and in our relationship. We were on the same playing field, and this made us thankful and more understanding and loving toward one another.

After dating for about a year, it became obvious we wanted to spend the rest of our lives together. Walking on a nature trail, I listened to the birds chirp and speak to one another. Nature is the most amazing place where I hear the Lord the most. Next to the waves at the beach, I saw, heard, and felt God and his presence. I loved being out in the nature just experiencing his creation. Turning to Brent as he stopped on the trail surrounded by the trees, flowers, and meadows, he bent down on one knee. "Will you marry me?" he asked. "WHAT! HERE?" I shrieked. I was astonished. I knew we talked about getting married, but a lot of our family members thought us too young to be married. "Yes!" I ultimately answered. I was promised to the Lord first and foremost, but I was ecstatic to be engaged to not only my best friend but also the love of my life.

*****

Standing in a tall steel building, the room was dark, gray, and filling with water. Turning to Brent, I was scared. I was consumed by fear and had no idea why. Looking around the room, I saw another person, boy, almost like a child in the room with us. I didn't know who he was, just that he was the source of my fear and where we were. Looking out of the glass window of the building, I saw the sky alight with fire. The sky was burning red with stormy clouds. The sea that surrounded the building on all sides twisted, churned, and raged around us.

Looking at the one wall of the building, I saw a laundry chute-like tunnel to slide out of the building. Turning to Brent I said I was scared. Looking at me, he replied he would go first and be with me. He slid down first, then me. Being dumped into the sea, I felt the fear, anxiety, and negative energy leave me. Standing on the beach with Brent, we jumped in celebration, happiness, and felt free.

*****

"I baptize you in the name of the Father, Son, and the Holy Spirit." Being dipped into the water, I became baptized along with Brent for the second time. Brent and I interpreted my dream as a message from God on how he wanted us to become baptized again. After running from him so many times after my first baptism, I was delighted to obey this command. I wanted to be baptized once more because this meant I could clean myself and receive the Holy Spirit once more.

*****

Present day

As I write this now, Brent and I have been married for almost six years. We are blessed with a beautiful baby girl, Elena, and are hoping for one more. I am still very much in contact with Michael, my first-born, and am blessed that I am able to have a relationship with him. Looking back, I knew I was not ready. I saw other single moms and knew I was not ready. I would have no support system or even a home for Michael. Herald, Tami, and I tell Michael I am the mommy who had him in his tummy; and Herald and Tami are his real mommy and daddy. The most spectacular thing that we heard from him when Herald and Tami told him I was pregnant with Elena was first, "Yay, I have a baby sister!" and second, "I am glad Sam has Brent to help her because she didn't have anyone to help her with me." We are so blessed to have a Lord who can show Michael why I did adoption.

Next, I want to say to all those who may have felt the way I did when I was going through my depression: Depression is a real thing. I needed help, and I felt like I had no support system or could even reach out for help. I tell you now though that I was wrong. First and for most, God is always with us. Call out to him, and he will be there with no doubt! Next, reach out to a counselor, brother, sister, friend, teacher, or even your pastor. That is what they are there for. You are worth it! God would not have personally handcrafted you with love if you were not meant to be here.

Next, I forgave all my family members for everything that happened in my life. There was so much pain on my end, but they were going through things too. Money is a real problem in our broken world. We are not supposed to fixate on or idolize money; however, when you're a parent with five or six children, and you do not have money or God in your life, you tend to react coldly. Unfortunately, it not only affects the parent on how they react but also the children.

Which was a big part of why my parents were cold, drinking, and abusive. But I forgive them, forgot, and pray for them.

Looking back on my short life, I have come to realize that God has been there for me the whole time. Even as I pushed God away and ran away from him, he was there with me throughout all my good times and hardships. We humans are simply that, humans. We mess up, make mistakes, and spiral downward. We cannot beat ourselves up for the mistakes that we make. The mistakes that we make only make us stronger and prepare for the next time another opportunity that we know is not good for us arises. When we do fall down, God is there reaching for us. He is lending us a hand to help us back up and into his warm embrace.

God blessed us with free will. Now this can be a blessing but also a curse. Free will means that we can choose which path to take. However, by choosing a path that God does not approve of such as stealing, drugs, murder, and so on and so forth, we choose to put ourselves in harm's way. We torture ourselves by thinking we know what is best for us.

> I am the resurrection and the life, he that belie-
> veth in me though he were dead yet shall he live,
> and who so ever liveth and believeth in me shall
> never die. Does thou believeth in this? (John
> 11:25–26 KJV)

God doesn't want us to torture ourselves. God knows what is best for our lives. He has a better plan for us than we ourselves can plan. He knows everything and is surprised by nothing. Choices that we may make, he already knows about; and situations that we may get ourselves into that are bad, he turns them into good. Now I know that sometimes this is hard to believe. Some may question just as I did—how did cutting myself and falling into a deep depression turn to be good? I tell you this: After my deep depression, cutting myself and trying to commit suicide, my parents enrolled all of us kids into youth group. They thought this would help my depression. Not only did it help my depression, but I became a Christian and earned a place in heaven.

The years to follow when I disobeyed God, did as I wanted, and tortured myself through all the events that took place afterward—all these led me to who I am today. As hard as my past is, I am thankful of who I am today. I am a follower of Christ, I have a big heart and love everyone whom I meet, and I met the man of my dreams. God had used all my hardships that I placed myself into and transformed me into the wonderful woman that I am today.

How do we know what God's will is? Well, as a wise pastor once said to me, only you can determine what God is telling you. However, there are many ways in which God speaks to us.

God can speak to us through many different opportunities. These ways can consist of an actual voice speaking to you, actions or words spoken through others to you, or feelings from our hearts of what to know or do or say. God also speaks through dreams as noted in previous chapters, as well as the Bible. God uses many different opportunities to speak to everyone. The biggest challenge is discernment. God does not condemn with hateful words, doubt, anxiety, or fear. He speaks through love, kindness, joy. Someone I have come to view as a mentor taught me three questions to ask when discerning God, his will for us, and his voice. Is it holy? Is it wise? And does it bring others closer to God? I like these three little questions because it can give you clarity when trying to discern God's will. Most of all pray! God wants us to have that relationship with him and wants us to pray for *everything*! So pray and invite him into your decision-making.

As I wrote this book, I was driven by fear, anxiety, and shame because of my past and who may read this. Since then, I have grown, transformed, and trusted God that the reason why he called me to write this book was not to air out my past but rather use it to help others. I am thankful to the Lord for showing me wonderful things continuously. He is always there when I am near and even when I run away. No one is perfect, and we may fall from time to time, but God is always there. God bless you all, and I pray that you will find the miracle that is Jesus. Through him, we find God and eternal life (John 14:6 NLT).

About the Author

Samantha Wooler is a behavioral therapist working in schools and the surrounding areas in homes of individuals diagnosed with disabilities. Currently, she is a stay-at-home mom and wife taking care of Elena, her one-and-a-half-year-old. She enjoys reading (some would call her a bookworm); writing; and spending time with her husband, Brent, and their child, Elena. Samantha is inspired to help those with disabilities due to having a disability herself, and she understands the challenges that not only the individual may face but also how it impacts the family. She feels blessed with what the Lord has given her in her lifetime and continues to worship and cherish her Lord and Savior.

CPSIA information can be obtained
at www.ICGtesting.com
Printed in the USA
LVHW020151290921
698984LV00001B/68